BIZARRE new orleans

...what the other guidebooks won't tell you.

st. eXpedite press

New Orleans

St. Expedite Press
P. O. Box 741021
New Orleans LA 70174

ISBN: 0-9652052-3-1

Library of Congress Card Catalog Number: 97-67378

Softcover: $6.95
Use ISBN when ordering.

COVER: Charles T. Howard mausoleum, Metairie Cemetery

TABLE OF CONTENTS

CEMETERIES

BOONDOCKS (outside the Quarter)

INSIDE OF THE CITY

OUTSIDE THE CITY

CHALMETTE

MUSIC & LITERATURE

ETC.

INTRODUCTION

No other city in North America is as diverse as New Orleans. Its history speaks for itself. The Indians were the first of course, followed by the French, the Spanish, then the Americans.

But it didn't stop there.

African Americans make up a majority of the city, followed by Italians, Irish, and more recently, Asian Americans. Hence came the influences of the Catholic Church, the Napoleonic Code, voodoo, etc, which inspired such things as Mardi Gras, jazz, St. Joseph's Day, the Underwear balls......

Words are inadequate in describing the city. Above all, it is sensual in nature -- a place of smells, sights, noises... Most guidebooks and travel logs only skim the surface of this truly unique metropolis. The typical tourist is led by the hand from Jackson Square, through the French Quarter and possibly Uptown. They are never encourage to take the side streets and are often advised not to do so.

This book will help tourists discover the real N.O. Locals will find it informative as well. Of course, no work of this nature can cover everything, which is the great thing about New Orleans. Surprises await the visitor around every corner. Probably the most interesting thing about New Orleans however is that the real N.O. can't be found in the streets, or bricks, or buildings but only within the people. New Orleans is unique because the people who live here and have lived here are unique, not a melting pot but rather a smorgasbord of delights.

One final point. No one uses North, South, East or West when giving directions. In New Orleans the usual directions are uptown (west), downtown (east), toward the river (south) and toward the lake (north). Also, the Westbank is south of the French Quarter.

USING THIS GUIDE

BIZARRE NEW ORLEANS is not your typical travel guide. First, it assumes you are a seasoned traveler and know the ropes concerning the do's and don't's of visiting any large U.S. city. Second, it assumes you can navigate in unfamiliar territory using only a map and this guide. To use this guide you *will* need a good map, preferably one that's easy to open and close, such as GOUSHA'S FASTMAP of New Orleans (sold at Walden's Book Store). Of course, you can get free maps at the Louisiana Tourist Center located in the Pontalba Building. These are OK but some of them do not contain all the streets in the city.

BIZARRE NEW ORLEANS is not just for tourists. In fact, many of the attractions listed in this guide will be unfamiliar to even the most seasoned New Orleanian. Therefore, you will probably be on your own when it comes down to locating any specific attraction. To assist you, a photo has been included for each subject, usually showing the outside of the establishment or attraction, or something on the outside of the building.

This guide has been divided into various geographical and thematic sections. All the attractions in the French Quarter are listed in the same section and are in close proximity to one another (geographic). On the other hand, all of the attractions regarding Music & Literature have been listed in the same section but are *not* located near one another (thematic). The same is true for the other sections. An index has also been included to help you find areas of particular interest.

PRONUNCIATIONS

Because New Orleans was settled by a succession of various nationalities, there are numerous problems with regard to the proper pronunciation of streets and places. Some still retain the French pronunciation, others their Spanish and American versions. Probably the most controversial name is "New Orleans" itself. Surprisingly, the confusion can be attributed to the local denizens themselves. While the city itself is usually pronounced "NU OR-lee-uns" (accent on the capital letters), the parish (county) in which the city is incorporated (Orleans Parish) is usually pronounced "OR-LEENS." Of course, locals have a whole host of variations for the pronunciation of their own city, such as "NAWLINS," "NU AWLINS," and NU AW-lee-uns." Tourist however, are advised not to imitate the locals. Why? Because they may think you are trying to make fun of them. Instead, listen to the local news programs and use the same pronunciations. You'll probably be safe. On the other hand, locals do expect you to know how to say street names. For example, if you say "DECK-a-tur," instead of "duh-KAY-tur," (Decatur) you will get funny looks from a lot of people.

FRENCH QUARTER STREETS

*Chartres -- CHAR-TERS
*Dauphine --DAW-feen
*Iberville -- EYE-burr-ville
*Conti -- CON-tie
*Dumaine -- DOO-main
*Esplanade -- S-plun-aid

*Bourbon -- BURR-bun
*Burgundy --burr-GUN-dee
*Bienville --BEE-in-ville
*Toulouse -- TA-loose
*Ursulines -- UR-sa-len

OTHERS

*Pontchartrain --PONCH-a-train
*Elysian Fields -- ee-LEE-shun
*Tchoupitoulas--CHOP-a-too-lus

*Baronne -- ba-RHONE
*Carondelet --ka-RON-du-let
*Claiborne -- CLAY-BORN

OTHER STREET CURIOSITIES

Many of the street names in New Orleans are puzzling, difficult to pronounce, and defy explanation. Nevertheless, as in most cities, most of the streets are named after prominent citizens or noted historical figures. A few however deserve mentioning.

DUMAINE, TOULOUSE, CONTI (French Quarter)
Early French residents were highly amused when they landed in New Orleans and discovered several streets named after the bastard sons of Louis XIV.

CHEF MENTEUR (New Orleans East)
Translated from French, it means "chief liar," which was what the Indians called Governor Kerlerec (1753-1763).

CHARLMARK (New Orleans East)
Named for Karl Marx, of the COMMUNIST MANIFESTO.

RAMPART STREET (French Quarter)
At one time an actual rampart (fortified wall) existed here, hence the name. The purpose of the wall was to protect the city from Indians, slave rebellions, the British, and other troublemakers. Not exactly the Great Wall of China, it mostly consisted of sticks.

O'REILLY (Gentilly)
Probably the most hated man in Louisiana history (besides General Butler). O'Reilly executed the ringleaders of a "rebellion" against the Spanish government. For the Creoles, naming a street after O'Reilly makes about as much sense as naming a street after Benedict Arnold. Then again, this is New Orleans.

MONA LISA DRIVE
A remote, gravel road ("Lover's Lane") in City Park. Supposedly, the ghost of a once-wronged unattractive woman (but with a nice smile) appears here when the moon is full and kills a young man out with his girl, then throws his body in the lagoon.

TCHOUPITOULAS (Uptown)
Somehow, the name was derived from the choupique fish.

PIRATE'S ALLEY (French Quarter)
So named in the 1830's. Why notorious pirates would hang out in an alley next to the church, the jail and the seat of government defies explanation.

FRENCH QUARTER

INTRODUCTION

The French Quarter is also called the Vieux Carre, which means the "Old Square." If you look at a map of the Quarter however, you can see that it is not even close to being a square. In fact, it's approx. twice as long as it is wide. Nevertheless, the name has persisted.

After the Civil War, most prominent Creoles began leaving the Quarter and by the 1920's, it had fallen into decay and soon became the home of immigrants. The closing of Storyville gave rise to the emergence of Bourbon Street as the focal point of the Vieux Carre. In 1936, the Vieux Carre Commission was created, whose function was to preserve the "quaint and distinctive character" of the district.

In 1961, a book (NEW ORLEANS, by Griffin) proclaimed "although the Quarter today is being reclaimed in all areas, progress is slow in the western section, around Dauphine and Burgundy. It is still possible to find cottages with no plumbing." As of 1996, the process is still incomplete. One might see just about anything in the Quarter. The grand and grotesque exist side by side. Nevertheless, over the years, property values have sky-rocketed and the Quarter is once again the "heart and soul" of New Orleans.

1000 BLOCK OF TOULOUSE

FRENCH QUARTER

ST LOUIS CATHEDRAL
JACKSON SQUARE

St. Louis Cathedral is not only a place of worship but a burial ground as well. Many historical figures rest here, such as Don Almonaster, who is responsible (monetarily speaking) for all the buildings surrounding Jackson Square.

The different churches at this site have suffered through various calamities. The first structure was destroyed by a hurricane (1723). The second church was struck by lightning (1781) and destroyed by fire (1788). The third and present structure has collapsed (1851), been cannonballed (1862), bombed (1919) and subjected to yearly flooding by the Mississippi. Although it has been refurbished several times, the Cathedral has not been completely rebuilt since 1794.

Formerly, the pews in the front of the church were auctioned off to the highest bidder. Those who did not pay up were subject to prosecution.

DIRECTIONS

Go to Jackson Square. If you can't find Jackson Square you shouldn't be using this guide and you shouldn't be walking around New Orleans.

ST. LOUIS CATHEDRAL

CABILDO
JACKSON SQUARE

The Cabildo is probably the most historic structure in the entire Mississippi Valley. It is now a museum but formerly served in many capacities. The museum contains many curious wonders, such as Napoleon's death mask and the only known portrait of Jean Lafitte. Anyone interested in the Civil War will no doubt find it informative, including the display on African Americans who fought on the side of the Confederacy. The Marquis de Lafayette lived in the Cabildo for a time and the block-buster case, Plessy vs. Ferguson (that separate but equal with regard to race was constitutional), was decided here .

The Arsenal and the Calabozo are now a part of the museum. The Arsenal was taken over by rebellious factions on several occasions during Reconstruction during the attempt to end carpetbag rule. The Calabozo (jail) was built in 1769 and at one time housed Pierre Lafitte for a short while before he escaped. The entrance to the old Calabozo is located on Pirate's Alley.

NAPOLEON'S DEATH MASK

FRENCH QUARTER

NUNEZ HOUSE
619 CHARTRES STREET

On March 21, 1788, Good Friday, a devotion candle in the house of Don Vincente Nunez (619 Chartres) caught the curtains on fire. The fire spread quickly and soon engulfed the entire city. Supposedly, the fire spread because on Good Friday, in the Catholic tradition, bells are not allowed to ring, which prevented the firemen from sounding the alarm.

The fire burned out of control for most of the day, destroying nearly 900 buildings, including the Cathedral, Cabildo, and most government buildings.

Six years later, on December 8, 1794, another devastating fire erupted. 40 city blocks were wiped out. The fire began at 534 Royal.

Governor Carondolet (Spanish), seeking the prevention of further disasters, enacted a new building code, which mandated the use of bricks, plastered and stuccoed walls, and tiled roofs. While it is true that the building code change greatly affected the look of the city, the basic architecture of the city remained French. There is no record of any Spanish architects ever living in New Orleans. Although many guidebooks tout New Orleans' Spanish architecture, there is no historical evidence to support its existence.

619 Chartres Street

ORLEANS BALLROOM
717 ORLEANS

Much has been made about the infamous Quadroon Balls.

To New Orleans Creoles however, there was nothing special about them. They were dances, pick-up places, where a white man could pick up a black woman. That was the extent of it.

Most of the time, nothing much resulted from the brief union. Sometimes however, the women were "set-up" with accommodations or an apartment. To outsiders however, the quadroon balls were seen as exotic, elaborate, foreign, --- and erotic. Basically though, the arrangements and circumstances were no different than that of any other mistress of any given time or place.

The "balls" were held all over the city, at various times and places, in the early to mid-1800's. Folklore has it that the Orleans Ballroom was one of the most popular spots. Whether this is true or not is debatable. In any case, the balls declined in popularity after the 'Americanization" of New Orleans.

Ironically, this same site was later to become an orphanage for mulatto children.

717 ORLEANS

COMMEMORATIVE
PLAQUE

FRENCH QUARTER

GARDETTE-LEPRETRE HOUSE
716 DAUPHINE

Beauregard was one of the most controversial figures in American history, in more ways than one. He started the Civil War, by ordering the bombardment of Fort Sumpter. Gen. Beauregard sent part of the captured flagstaff from Ft. Sumpter to this address, where it was presented to the Orleans Guards.

Beauregard refused to attend the funeral of Jeff Davis, simply because he didn't like him. After the War, he was hired as a front man for the Louisiana Lottery, receiving $30,000 a year for working one hour a week. The Lottery was located at the corner of St. Charles and Union. Two blindfolded boys overseen by Beauregard made daily, semi-monthly and semi-annual drawings. It was the largest gambling operation ever to exist prior to the 20th century. It controlled newspapers, banks and politicians for over 20 years. The Grand prize ($600,000) was never won.

The Beauregard Keyes House (1113 Chartres), were Beauregard lived for a short time, is supposedly haunted.

So is 716 Dauphine, constructed in 1836.

Previous to the construction of the existing house, a wealthy Turkish "Sultan" had occupied the old premises in 1727. After hearing screams in the night, neighbors found the Turk buried alive in his garden and his harem murdered. Shortly thereafter, and up until the present, residents have reported mysterious footsteps, screams and ghosts.

716 DAUPHINE

FRENCH QUARTER

HOUSE OF THE RISING SUN
826-830 ST. LOUIS

Prior to the opening of Storyville in 1897, prostitution in the Crescent City flourished nevertheless, mainly in the French Quarter. Although most of these houses are unknown and forgotten, one remains famous, even to this day -- The House of the Rising Sun. To most of us in the late 20th century, the song, The House of the Rising Sun, is associated with The Animals, a rock group, who recorded it in 1965. It was first recorded in 1945 however, by Leadbelly. Leadbelly, a prolific song writer, also wrote such classics as Midnight Special, Rock Island Line, and Goodnight Irene. Leadbelly, whose real name was Huddie Ledbetter, was born in Louisiana, near Shreveport. In 1918 he was sent to prison in Texas for murder, but pardoned by the governor of Texas in 1925, after the governor heard him sing. In 1930 he was again sentenced to prison, for intent to murder, this time in Louisiana. He was discovered by John Lomax, who was traveling around the U.S. recording folk artists. Lomax initially recorded Leadbelly while he was in prison. Leadbelly was later pardoned by the governor of Louisiana in 1933. Leadbelly went on to become famous by touring the U.S. and singing his original songs and died in 1949.

The House of the Rising Sun was so named for its madam -- Madam Marianne LeSoleil Levant (which means rising sun, when translated from French). The house was open for business from 1862 (when New Orleans was under occupation by Union troops) until 1874, when it was closed because of complaints by neighbors.

One question remains however, If the house was closed in 1874, and Leadbelly was not born until 1888, how could he have written the lyrics?

826 ST. LOUIS

FRENCH QUARTER

AUDUBON COTTAGE
505 DAUPHINE

Despite the eventual popularity of *Birds of America,* Audubon had a difficult time getting the project off the ground.

In 1819, at the age of 34, he lost all his money through bad investments, was jailed, and forced to declare bankruptcy. In 1820 he set out for New Orleans on a Mississippi flatboat as a deckhand. Along the way he lost all his drawings and arriving in New Orleans lost all of his money at the hands of a pickpocket. His drawings continued to be unpopular and he was forced to do portraits on the side to make a living. On one occasion he was paid $120 for a nude drawing. When it was completed, the model signed her own name to the drawing and swore him to secrecy concerning the portrait.

Audubon was ambidextrous and could draw with both hands at once, working up to 14 hours a day. In 1821 his wife and son joined him in New Orleans but he and his son soon contracted yellow fever. While his wife taught school John continued to earn his living by doing portraits, giving flute lessons, dancing lessons, and fencing instructions. Still unable to sell his idea to anyone in the U.S., he ventured to London, whereupon he found a publisher and an engraver and began selling subscriptions to his new portfolio of birds. Each portfolio consisted of 435 prints, each measuring 39.5" x 29.5" and sold for about $1,000. Today each set of the massive work is valued at approx. $2 million.

From 1821-1822, while working on the *Birds of America* series, Audubon lived at 505 Dauphine. The cottage is currently a part of the Maison de Ville Hotel complex, and can be rented.

505 DAUPHINE

LUCKY CHENG'S
720 ST. LOUIS STREET

From the outside, it appears to be a typical New Orleans restaurant. Lucky Cheng's however, is rather different, even for New Orleans. For one, the food is unique, an eclectic blend of Asian and Creole, that varies depending on the whims of the chef. Likewise with the desserts. Monika's Foot Fetish ($25) consists of a chocolate slipper filled with raspberry mousse.

Most people who visit though do not do so solely for the cuisine. Lucky Cheng's boosts that "reality is illusion and things aren't always what they seem."

Quite so.

The "waitresses" are drag queens and the staff consists entirely of transvestites and transsexuals. Monday night at 9:00 p.m. usually features a drag show, while the second floor banquet room caters to private parties for special occasions.

Reservations are advised.

720 ST. LOUIS

TIPS

If you are looking for a nice quiet place for dinner for two, this should probably not be your first choice. On Friday and Saturday nights, things can get a little rowdy, so be prepared.

FRENCH QUARTER

D. H. HOLMES
819 CANAL STREET

D. H. Holmes Department Store, formerly located at 819 Canal St, was the first department store in America. It was also the first department store to hire women. D. H. Holmes was purchased by Dillard Department Stores and closed in 1989. This location is noted for three things: 1) the clock, 2) Ignatius Reilly, and 3) the Footstomper.

The D. H. Holmes clock was put up in 1913 and for many generations of New Orleanians, served as an initial meeting place for friends venturing anywhere downtown -- until it mysteriously disappeared one night. It wasn't until April 1995 that the mystery was finally solved, when two Kenner men confessed. At 10:30 p.m. on May 17, 1989 they had set up a ladder, cut the wires, removed the 8 bolts holding it up and absconded with the prized possession.

In A CONFEDERACY OF DUNCES by John K. Toole, the opening scene in the Pulitzer Prize winning novel occurs in front of the Holmes store, directly under the clock, as Ignatius Reilly is waiting for his mother.

This area was also terrorized by the Footstomper in the late 1980's. The Footstomper, who was never caught, patrolled Canal Street, looking for unsuspecting women. Upon choosing his victim, who was usually window shopping, the Footstomper would sneak up, suddenly stomp the victim's foot and disappear into the French Quarter.

819 CANAL ST.

CUSTOM HOUSE
423 CANAL

The **CUSTOM HOUSE**, constructed of Massachusetts granite, has walls that are approximately 4 feet thick. It was begun in 1848 and was not finished until 1881. Construction was halted during the Civil War and work resumed in 1871. Inside, the fourth floor remains unfinished.

The choice of granite is puzzling. Granite is a particularly heavy stone and not conducive to construction in swampy, south Louisiana. Consequently, the corner stone is currently about 6 feet below ground and sinking.

General Butler, who occupied New Orleans during the Civil War, used this building as his headquarters. The second story was used as a prison for Confederate prisoners. The Custom House was also used by Louisiana Governor Kellog in 1874 as a retreat during the Battle of Liberty Place.

Although some find the structure interesting, Mark Twain said it reminded him of a large icebox.

**CUSTOM HOUSE
CLINTON STREET ENTRANCE**

FRENCH QUARTER

OLD ABSINTHE HOUSE
238 BOURBON STREET

This historical structure is located at 238 Bourbon and should not be confused with the Absinthe Bar, located just down the street. While both establishments are noteworthy, the Old Absinthe House is the more famous, for several reasons. Patrons of the OAH have included Mark Twain, Oscar Wilde, Walt Whitman, Jenny Lind, Aaron Burr, Andy Jackson, Lafayette, William Taft, Teddy Roosevelt and O. Henry, just to name a few. The OAH is also famous for its secret room, where, supposedly, Jackson and Lafitte planned the Battle of New Orleans (others say it was at Maspero's Exchange -- 440 Chartres)

Absinthe, a 100-180 proof drink containing anise and wormwood, was banned in 1912. Wormwood is an addictive, hallucinogenic liquid squeezed from the roots of a small bush. For 22 years after the ban the New Orleans Absinthe Manufactures produced absinthe without the wormwood. In 1934 it too was banned by federal law.

238 BOURBON STREET

EXCHANGE ALLEY

This dark, narrow alleyway has seen better days, especially the 100 block (Exchange Place). Even so, its worth the detour.

At the corner of Canal and Exchange Alley, where now sits the home of the Whopper, once sat the first motion picture theatre in the United States, Vitascope Hall. For 10 cents one could enter and watch such "movies" as The Kiss. For another 10 cents one could peek inside the projectionist's booth. And for another dime one could take home a souvenir, a single frame of exposed celluloid. Vitascope Hall operated for three months in 1896.

111 Exchange Place, designed by Gallier in 1866, doesn't appear to be significant at first glance. But the 5 story building contains a rare cast iron front, which was a significant development in American building technology. The building is easily distinguished by its Venetian Renaissance style Corinthian columns.

Lee Harvey Oswald lived at 126 Exchange Place at Mack's Apartments, while attending Beauregard Junior High School, and often hung out in the pool hall below his apartment. (See OSWALD p. 54)

During the 1830s and 1840s the 300 block of Exchange Alley was the site of many "academies" for dueling. Several were located at the corner of Conti and Exchange Alley. Pepe Llulla, the most famous instructor, fought 41 duels with no defeats. His favorite pastime was shooting an egg out of his son's hand at 50 paces.

EXCHANGE ALLEY, 300 BLOCK

FRENCH QUARTER

LALAURIE HOUSE
1140 ROYAL STREET

The most famous haunted house in the city is the La Maison Lalaurie at 1140 Royal. On April 10, 1834 a fire broke out in the kitchen and spread throughout the house. When firemen began inspecting the premises they discovered more than a dozen chained and bound slaves in the attic. Some were dead, others mutilated. Madame Lalaurie fled and was never seen again and the house remained vacant for years and fell into disrepair. Soon, rumors began to circulate about ghosts roaming the upper balcony and faces appearing in the attic windows.

Other French Quarter sites include:

-- 714 St. Peter. A cafe now where a victim of a sadistic dentist and a mysterious black cat haunts the establishment. (Coffee Pot Restaurant).
--- 711 Bourbon St. Penelope Tricou, who accidentally died in 1874 when she lost her footing and tumbled to her death, roams the premises.
-- 1303 Burgundy. Formerly a Spanish garrison where troops mutinied and were subsequently tortured and their bodies cemented inside one of the walls. Supposedly, a company of zombie soldiers walks out of the walls.
--- 734 Royal. The spirit of Julie, an octoroon (1/8 black) mistress, walks naked across the roof between midnight and dawn only during the month of December.
--- 1003 Bourbon St, Room #40. Lafitte Guest House. Supposedly haunted.

1140 ROYAL STREET

24

LAFITTE'S BLACKSMITH SHOP
941 BOURBON STREET

From all accounts, Jean Lafitte can best be described as an aquatic Jesse James. Although labeled as a pirate by most, he preferred the term "privateer." Legends abound about this mysterious figure, many concerning buried treasure. In 1813 Louisiana Gov. Claiborne issued a proclamation offering $500 for the pirate's capture. Lafitte countered with posters plastered all over the city, offering $1500 reward for Claiborne's capture. In the Battle of New Orleans, Lafitte cut a deal with Andrew Jackson, who agreed to intercede for Lafitte and his men in obtaining pardons. Soon after his pardon, Lafitte took to the seas again, from a new base on Galveston Island. Of Lafitte's later years little is known. Presumably, he died in the Yucatan in 1826.

Lafitte's Blacksmith Shop is one of the oldest buildings in the French Quarter. Legend has it that it was a front for selling smuggled goods and slaves. On the other hand, the Lafitte brothers boldly maintained a shop on Royal Street and advertised in the press whenever an auction was to be held from their warehouses in Barataria. Regarding slaves, there was no point in hiding the fact. The notarial records of the time are filled with thousands of slaves sold by Pierre Lafitte.

Two other facts about Jean Lafitte are of particular note. One, he never fought in the Battle of New Orleans. His men did, such as Dominique You, but Jean remained on a ship in the Mississippi River for the entire battle. Two, although Jean is remembered as a hero, in later life he actually turned against the United States and acted as a spy for Spain.

941 BOURBON STREET

FRENCH QUARTER

SHAW RESIDENCE
1313 DAUPHINE ST

In December 1966 Clay Shaw was summoned down to District Attorney Jim Garrison's office to answer a few questions. Two months later Garrison charged him with conspiracy to assassinate JFK. The resulting trial, as depicted in Oliver Stone's movie JFK (1993), was by all accounts a complete farce. Nevertheless, it ruined the reputation of Shaw, a prominent businessman (associated with the International Trade Mart). In the trial Garrison alleged that Clay was a homosexual. While the jury found him not guilty of conspiracy, Shaw remained marred by the sexual stigma.

Clay wasn't the only one smeared by the publicity however. In February 1970 Jack Anderson accused Jim Garrison of molesting a 13 year old boy in 1969. Likewise, the judge in the Shaw trial, Edward Haggerty, was arrested in December 1969 in a vice raid during a stag show in a motel room.

Clay Shaw died in 1974 at the age of 61. At the time of the Garrison investigation he lived in the French Quarter at 1313 Dauphine. A plaque erected in his memory is located in the 700 block of Gov. Nicholls.

1313 DAUPHINE ST.

FRENCH QUARTER

OLD U.S. MINT
400 ESPLANADE AVENUE

One of the most historic buildings in the city. It was here in 1815 that General Andrew Jackson assembled and reviewed his troops before departing to the battlefield at Chalmette. (Jackson, who was anxious to get as many men as possible, instigated various methods for obtaining recruits and munitions. The deal he cut Lafitte was widely known. To entice "free men of color," however, he offered them land and money. While the Governor of Louisiana (Claiborne) had no objection to cutting deals with cutthroats and pirates, he was strongly against the latter and balked at the idea for over one month before agreeing.)

After General Farragut captured the city in 1862, General Benjamin F. Butler headed the Union Army of Occupation. When William Mumfrey tore down the U.S. flag which was flying over the Mint, he was subsequently hung by General Butler. Accordingly, he was hung at the scene of the crime.

Besides U.S. coins, the Confederate States of America Half-Dollar, one of the rarest coins in the world, was also minted here. Its production was authorized by Jeff Davis in early 1861. Only 4 of the coins were ever struck and the existence of the coins remained largely unknown until 1879 when the coins and both dies were discovered in the possession of B.F. Taylor of New Orleans. When the coins were originally struck, one was given to Jeff Davis, where it remained in his possession until he was captured by Union forces (see Cemeteries -- Army of Northern Virginia).

Currently, the Mint houses several collections, including a Jazz Museum.

400 BLOCK OF
ESPLANADE

27

FRENCH QUARTER

GALLATIN STREET

Currently, Bourbon Street is where one goes for a little action, tourists and locals alike. Before that, it was Storyville. Before Storyville was Gallatin Street, which existed from 1840-1870.

By all accounts, it was a rough place. Nicknamed the "Street of a Thousand Murders," it consisted of dance halls, gin mills and brothels. Needless to say, the police were afraid to venture in after dark. Consequently, once off the street and inside the establishments, just about anything went. Gambling was also popular, with animal fights the norm, including dog and rat battles.

On many occasions, men were never seen or heard from again after entering one of the many shanties that lined both sides of the street. As for the women, one can vividly imagine what lay in store for them. But venture forth they did, usually paying the consequences. On one occasion for example, a certain woman named Annie was stabbed and beaten with her own wooden leg at the Green Tree bar (a 3 story building located 2 doors down from Barracks Street).

Gallatin Street is now the 1100-1200 block of French Market Place and features a flea market.

FRENCH MARKET PLACE

INTRODUCTION

Over the years numerous theories have been developed to explain the prevalence of the aboveground tomb. Ask any New Orleanian and the typical explanation is "because New Orleans is below sea level," meaning that one always encounters ground water when digging below sea level. Though reasonable, this answer is not quite accurate. Death Valley for example is below sea level, 282 feet below sea level, and there's not much water there.

A simpler explanation exists. The New Orleans tomb evolved for the same reason that the skyscraper evolved in crowded cities. In old New Orleans, land was scarce. To economize on space and land, N.O. did not dig down but instead built up. Today New Orleanians continue to use the tomb system mainly for traditional and nostalgic reasons.

The cemeteries play an important role in the Roman Catholic culture of New Orleans. It doesn't rival Mardi Gras but All Saint's Day is a festive occasion in New Orleans and a legal holiday. Whole families venture out to the cemeteries carrying picnic baskets, flowers, camcorders, brooms, and weedeaters to honor the dead. There is some mystery however concerning the origin of this ritual and its significance. In other sections of the country graves are decorated and adorned on Memorial Day and All Soul's Day. Southern Louisiana is the only area where this occurs on All Saint's Day, November 1, the day preceding All Soul's Day.

DIRECTIONS

For the location of cemeteries see the table at the end of the index.

ST. LOUIS III CEMETERY

CEMETERIES

HOWARD MAUSOLEUM
METAIRIE CEMETERY

Charles T. Howard was blackballed from membership in the Metairie Jockey Club (which owned the Metairie Racetrack) all because he showed up at the club in shirt sleeves.

In a fit of anger, he shouted he would make a cemetery out of their racetrack.

Along with several others, including the President of the Racing Association, Howard kept his word. The Metairie Cemetery Association was granted a charter in 1872 and the first interment took place in 1873.

Within the Howard mausoleum sits a mysterious marble figure, beckoning for silence.

TIPS

A map of the cemetery is available at the Lake Lawn/Metairie Funeral Home office. A 60 minute cassette tape (self-guided tour) is also available at the office. Use of the tape is free, but you must leave a driver's license as a security deposit.

HOWARD MAUSOLEUM

MASICH TOMB
METAIRIE CEMETERY

On Avenue H in Section 83, just down from the information office, you will find the Masich tomb. In front of this tomb on the sidewalk, you will see a dog, a big white dog with a ribbon around its neck. A large tear hangs from his eye.

Legend has it that the dog followed his master's coffin to the tomb and would not leave. When removed, he always returned. Finally, he died from loneliness. A statue was placed at the door of the tomb as a tribute to the animal's devotion and faithfulness.

At frequent intervals, flowers appear, along with a new ribbon. A card is also left with the words, "to a good dog." Nevertheless, no one has ever been seen at the tomb.

MASICH TOMB

CEMETERIES

METAIRIE CEMETERY
BRUNSWIG TOMB

According to historians, it was Napoleon's expedition to Egypt (1798) that reawakened the public's interest in Egyptology. As a result the obelisk, pyramid and the pylon became incorporated into European and American architecture. One of the outstanding examples of this rejuvenated interest is the Brunswig pyramid in Metairie.

In recent years a certain mystique has again arisen concerning pyramids. According to adherents of pyramidology, they possess mysterious electrical forces -- which may explain things. The Brunswig tomb was once struck by a bolt of blue lightning which dislodged some of the upper stones without disturbing the large apex stone at the very top. Precariously balanced, but completely intact, it hung for several days as if suspended by the powers within, until workers could fashion it back together.

BRUNSWIG TOMB

DIRECTIONS

The Brunswig tomb is located at the circle on the western end of Avenue D.

32

BRUNSWIG TOMB (continued)
METAIRIE CEMETERY

New Orleans has always been obsessed with Egyptology. From its architecture, to its cemeteries, to its way of live, the Crescent City has much in common with its sister city. For example,

1) Cairo and New Orleans are both situated at the heads of great rivers.

2) They are both located on the same latitude, 30N.

3) Both experience mild, sunny winters and long, hot summers.

4) Cairo has an old quarter, with narrow streets and over-hanging balconies. New Orleans has the same thing in the French Quarter.

5) Prior to the Civil War, cotton was a leading export of N.O. As a result of the war and a union blockade of New Orleans, Great Britain was cut off from American cotton. Consequently, Britain turned to Egypt, which soon began supplying the British textile industry. Today, cotton is still one of Egypt's most important crops, much of it shipped through Cairo.

6) Both cities contain "cities of the dead," which are frequented once a year. In Cairo, it occurs at the end of Ramadan, when family members "who can no longer wear new clothes" are paid a visit.

7) Both cities contain sections called faubourgs.

8) The main part of New Orleans is located on the East Bank. Ditto for Cairo.

DETAIL, BRUNSWIG TOMB

CEMETERIES

JEFFERSON DAVIS
METAIRIE CEMETERY

Davis died in New Orleans on Dec 6, 1889. His entombment in the Army of N. Virginia mausoleum was to be temporary, pending a decision on his final resting place. On the day of the funeral (Dec. 11) all schools were closed. Business was suspended and all government offices were closed. The casket was placed on a flower-decorated caisson and the procession formed a long march. It took 3 ½ hours to cover the route and more than 10,000 persons gathered at the cemetery. After a lengthy service the crypt was sealed with a marble tablet on which the signature of Davis was engraved. On May 31, 1893, the coffin was moved to Richmond VA. The tablet was sealed in place once more and the crypt in Metairie never used again.

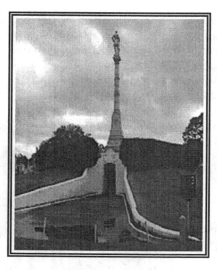

Although Davis was revered and respected by all Southerners, he was never able to live down the circumstances surrounding his capture. Davis was captured in Georgia on May 10, 1865. In his report to the War Department Union General James Wilson reported that Jeff Davis had tried to escape by putting on a dress-- one of Mrs. Davis' dresses. At first the Union troops thought he was a woman. Noticing his boots however, Davis was soon caught and identified.

ARMY OF N. VA. MAUSOLEUM

DIRECTIONS

This mausoleum is located near the Brunswig tomb, at the center of the circle at the western end of Avenue D.

ARMY OF NORTHERN VIRGINIA MAUSOLEUM
METAIRIE CEMETERY

New Orleans is an important burial ground for many adherents of the Confederacy. After the war, thousands came to the city, forming associations of veterans of the different armies. These groups, similar to the modern day V.F.W. provided services to its members, including burial in some of the tombs maintained by the group. In Metairie there are four such memorials, three of which are among the most impressive Civil War monuments to be found. Probably the most impressive is the mausoleum of the Association Army of N. Virginia, Louisiana Division, occupying the large circle at the end of Avenues A & D. Atop the 40 foot granite column sits the heroic figure of General Thomas Jonathan Jackson, sculptured by N.O. artist Perelli.

With the exception of Robert E. Lee, no other character associated with the Civil War has attracted as much attention and fanfare as Jackson. Noted for his military conquests and battlefield genius, literally hundreds of anecdotes and stories have filtered their way down, including the legendary tale of how he acquired his name. What is not generally known however is that Stonewall was slain by his own troops, the fatal shots fired by men from the 18th North Carolina.

STONEWALL JACKSON

CEMETERIES

HENNESSY MONUMENT
METAIRIE CEMETERY

David C. Hennessy, Chief of Police for the City of New Orleans, was gunned down on October 15, 1890. On his way home (275 Girod St) that evening, he was ambushed at the corner Basin and Girod and died at 189 Basin (between Girod and Lafayette). Although Hennessey fired at the assailants, they fled and eluded capture.

The next day 38 Italians were arrested and detained. On October 19 Mayor Shakespeare delivered a special message to the City Council claiming that "beyond a shadow of a doubt Hennessey was the victim of Sicilian vengeance."

The case did not come to trial until February 28, 1891. 780 prospective jury members were examined before a jury could be seated. Nine were accused of murder, all Italians, but three were subsequently dismissed. On March 13, the jury brought in a verdict of "mistrial as to three, and acquittal for the rest."

On March 14 a huge mob gathered at the Henry Clay statue, marched to Congo Square and stormed the prison. Eleven men were lynched, the six who had been on trial and five others. Its work completed, the mob dispersed in an orderly fashion and made their way home.

HENNESSY MONUMENT

MORIARTY MONUMENT
METAIRIE CEMETERY

Located at the old main entrance stands one of the tallest privately owned monuments in the United States. Originally created for Mary Moriarty and completed in 1914, it also contains the remains of Daniel Moriarty, her husband.

Upon arrival in New Orleans from Vermont, it was discovered that it was too big to be moved on the local railroads, so a new railroad track had to be laid directly to the cemetery. After the first erecting firm went bankrupt, a second was hired. When Mr. Moriarty demanded that the contractor straighten out the cross, the second contractor also went bankrupt.

Mrs. Moriarty's will stipulated that only the date of her death be shown. This was done except that the stonecutter inscribed the wrong date, which was never changed, as Mr. Moriarty did not want to part with an extra $2.50.

Popular folklore has it that the four life-size statues represent the four virtues -- Faith, Hope, Charity, and Mrs. Moriarty.

LAGNIAPPE

If the monument were erected today, it would cost approx. $1,000,000.

MORIARTY MONUMENT

CEMETERIES

MARIE LAVEAU
SAINT LOUIS I

Located just outside the French Quarter, St. Louis I, the oldest existing cemetery in New Orleans, is a haphazard maze of ovens, family vaults, and society tombs. Twenty paces from the entrance sits the Paris tomb, recognized as the resting place of Marie Laveau. Marie was the daughter of Charles Laveau, a wealthy white planter, and Marquerite Henry, a quadroon (1/4 black). Marie married Jacques Paris, a free man of color, at age 36. When Paris died Marie became a hairdresser and lived with a man named Glapion, for whom she bore 15 children. Subsequently, she became the Voodoo Queen of New Orleans.

With the introduction of slaves in Louisiana, voodooism entered the daily lives of the citizens of New Orleans, both black and white. According to Lyle Saxon, author of FABULOUS NEW ORLEANS, the blacks took to it easily because of certain inborn traits. "It must be remembered," he says, "that he (the negro) is intensely emotional, possesses a childlike credulity, that his imagination is easily inflamed,

and that to him, the powers of darkness are potent powers." Later on, Saxon tells us that "It was not long before white men and women felt the power of voodoo and learned to fear it." Presumably, for different reasons than the excitable negroes.

There is some dispute over her final resting site, supposedly because there were two Marie Laveaus, mother and daughter. Some claim she is actually buried in St. Louis II, in an oven that also contains many red X's.

GLAPION TOMB

MARIE LAVEAU (continued)
SAINT LOUIS I

Marie did not popularize voodoo. In her time there were over 300 voodoos (practitioners) operating in the city. Given this, how did she make it to the top of the heap? The answer is simple. She rose to the top for the same reason that anyone rises to the top of their profession -- she was good at it. Using basic business and marketing techniques, she prospered.

Marie incorporated Christian rites and ceremonies into the Voodoo religion, making it more palatable, acceptable and therefore more effective. As a hairdresser for many years, she knew all the gossip in the community, knew who was sleeping with who, etc. She used this information to her advantage, playing one person against another. Showmanship and sex played an integral role in her ceremonies. Thinly-clad men and women, snakes, headless chickens, hypnotic drums and boiling kettles were all part of Marie's weekly show. Marie also tried to present a positive image of herself. She nursed the sick for free and visited prisoners. Using these and other techniques, Marie brought voodoo into the open, made it acceptable, and thereby profitable to herself. Basically, she was Louisiana's first great businesswoman.

Even more fascinating than Marie's life is her tomb. To this day it remains a living shrine. Adorned with fresh flowers, coins, pieces of brick, candles, folded slips of paper, sticks of incense, black feathers, and red X's, Marie's tomb is a revelation. It reminds one that some people have probably never heard of the quark, are not familiar with the laws of supply and demand, do not hold certain truths to be self-evident, and probably are not concerned with their cholesterol level. That people are different, believe in different things, and always will, regardless of the truth or facts.

GLAPION TOMB, DETAIL

CEMETERIES

ST. LOUIS II

For the past 15 years there has been talk of demolishing Saint Louis II Cemetery. Renovation has been considered but the cost is prohibitive. In 1974, the Archdiocese of New Orleans reported that it would cost over $1,000,000 to renovate the oven vaults alone.

Over the past few years this cemetery seems to have become the place of choice for those seeking to exercise the various freedoms granted by the Bill of Rights. Why they choose to perform them under cover of darkness is unknown, except by the practitioners. Various objects, including yellow boots, voodoo dolls, chicken carcasses, and bags of coconuts are continually cropping up. A walk through the cemetery confirms these findings. Besides the paraphernalia, one discovers crumbling, decrepit tombs, beer and whisky bottles, human bones and detects a slight odor in the air, regardless of the direction of the wind.

In order to give tourists the experience of the cemeteries without visiting them, one historical group, SAVE OUR CEMETERIES,

began working on a film to be shown in specific tourist centers. Members of the group, while conducting research, were held up at gunpoint and robbed of their cameras and equipment.

PLAQUE IN FRONT OF
ST. LOUIS II

RECOMMENDATIONS

Avoid this place! There is nothing here that you can't see at St. Louis I.

LAFAYETTE I

After St. Louis I, Lafayette I is probably the most frequently visited cemetery in the city. Probably because of its proximity to Commander's Palace, N.O.'s most famous restaurant. Also, it is within walking distance from the streetcar.

When the city of Lafayette was annexed by New Orleans in 1852, the cemetery also came under the providence of N.O. From there it went downhill. By the 1950's the foliage was so thick that one needed a machete to view the tombs. Some of the vaults had 15 foot trees growing on top. In 1969 a bond issue was passed to "improve" certain cemeteries throughout the city. This improvement included the planned destruction of many of the older vaults. Due to citizen involvement, most of the tombs were rebuilt and the main aisles replanted with magnolias. The cemetery was subsequently placed on the National Register of Historic Places.

On Friday the 13th, in June of 1980, a special ceremony was held in Lafayette I. A chartered flight from Houston TX brought the guests, who were all dressed in black. Four black limousines took the entourage to the cemetery. It was not a funeral however, but a wedding. The bride and groom, both previously married, told the caretaker they had come to bury the past.

In most cemeteries, including Lafayette I, cast iron is typically utilized in the fencing which surrounds many of the family plots. Lafayette I also contains wrought iron, which can be seen in the entrance gate.

OVEN VAULTS AT LAFAYETTE I

41

CEMETERIES

SOON ON TONG
CYPRESS GROVE

The Soon On Tong Association tomb in Cypress Grove was used as a receiving vault and temporary burial place for New Orleanians of Chinese descent. It contains a small fireplace which was used to burn incense and prayers written on paper. The individual vaults inside are labeled in Arabic numbers. At intervals of about 10 years the vaults were opened, the bones removed, packed into steel boxes, and shipped back to China.

The Chinese, like other nationalities, hold many traditional beliefs concerning death and burial. Just as in the U.S., customs vary, depending on a person's religion, status, and economic circumstances. In general however, great effort is made to return the body for burial in the ancestral graveyard. In the Buddhist ceremony, the priest sets off fireworks to chase away the devils. Prayers are written on rice paper by relatives and burned so that they can follow the spirit. Incense is burned and food, drink, tobacco, and money are placed near the deceased so that the spirit might refresh itself. Just like anywhere else, announcements are

sent out providing information concerning the arrangements. Typically, the age of death is generally exaggerated by 5 or 6 years because in China, only the bad die young.

Over the years, the custom of sending the remains back to China has largely been discontinued. Many Chinese have chosen to be buried in this country. In Metairie for example, the Tsoi tomb features individual granite containers for cinerary urns.

SOON ON TONG TOMB

42

ST. ROCH'S

For most saints it's hard to determine where fact ends and legend begins. For St. Roch (or Rock) it's extremely difficult because little is known of his personal life. Basically, he was a healer. When his parents died, he went to Rome and while in town, cured the Pope's brother. Thereafter, he was infected by the plague and not wishing to burden anyone, set out for the woods to die. There, he was miraculously fed by a dog until he recovered. Afterwards, he again began curing everyone in sight as well as their cattle. Later on he was imprisoned for being a spy and died shortly thereafter.

St. Roch's Cemetery contains a small Gothic chapel, housing an assortment of unique items. Replicas of human limbs and organs hang along the walls, testifying to the curing power of "The Rock." Beneath these, one sees stacks of crutches, braces, and artificial limbs. On the altar is a statue of St. Roch and his dog. This chapel was constructed by a Father Thevis's own hands around 1866 after his parishioners were spared the yellow fever raging the city.

St. Roch is also known for his power to cure ailing hearts. In former times, those seeking a good man, or those looking to get rid of a bad one, would often visit the cemetery. To get rid of a man required more than simple prayers however. One had to pick a rooster naked, give him a spoonful of whiskey, then put a piece of paper in his beak with the person's name written on it 9 times. If the rooster was then turned loose in the cemetery, the man was guaranteed to die within 3 days.

GATE, ST. ROCH'S CEMETERY

CEMETERIES

CHARITY

In more ways than one, Charity is not your typical New Orleans cemetery. From the Canal Street gate, no vaults are visible, no tombstones, no markers present. From all appearances it seems to be a small, unkept yard that someone has forgotten to mow.

Forgotten is correct.

The Mississippi runs deep but the ground beneath Charity runs even deeper. Below the surface lies the bodies of 60,000+ souls.

For years, Charity Hospital Cemetery has been the "big boneyard on the bayou," mainly from epidemics. During four days in September of 1847, this cemetery received 87 persons, mostly as a result of yellow fever.

Even among society's dregs, status has stepped in. For the destitute, those with nothing -- not even a name -- a distinction was made. Whites were placed up front near the street, blacks in the back, near the fence.

GATE, CHARITY CEMETERY

OFFNER MONUMENT
GATES OF PRAYER

Present day New Orleans maintains a large Jewish community. As a result, several Jewish cemeteries dot the city. Traditionally, burials are made below ground and simple headstones used, but not always. After receiving charitable aid from the Lighthouse for the Blind, Harry Offner chose to lie under this monument.

Judaism holds many other traditions relating to death and burial. According to Jewish tradition, when death occurs, the windows must be thrown open, mirrors covered or turned toward the wall, and garments rented (torn). After death, the body must never be left alone and a constant watch maintained. The bodies of women are attended only by women and the bodies of children must not be kissed.

It is of utmost importance that all must accompany the dead to the grave, even those who do not know the deceased. Anyone who sees a funeral procession is urged to join in for at least four paces. For obvious reasons, the only persons who are not required to join in the funeral procession are those in a wedding procession.

OFFNER MONUMENT

CEMETERIES

MCDONOGH

McDonogh Cemetery is located on the Westbank of the Mississippi River, near Gretna. Originally, it was established for his slaves. In 1850, McDonogh was buried near the center of the cemetery but his remains were later transferred to Baltimore. For many years the empty tomb was maintained by one of his former slaves.

More tales are told about McDonogh than either Andrew Jackson or Jean Lafitte. Many of them concern his miserly ways. Another concerns his love life. According to this story, after his sweetheart joined the convent, McDonogh withdrew to McDonoghville. There he spent the next 33 years in secluded poverty, moping in sorrow. Living as a recluse, he worked from dawn to midnight, never went outside, received no callers, did not read the newspaper, and hoarded all his money. On those rare occasions when he did opt to go out, he walked to save bus fare. When he had to go into New Orleans, he rowed across the river to save ferry fare.

When McDonogh died he was one of the wealthiest men in the city and left half his fortune to New Orleans , for educational purposes. His will stipulated that 1) the Bible had to be read once daily in N.O. public schools, 2) boys and girls from the 5th grade up had to be segregated, 3) the first Friday in May was to be proclaimed McDonogh Day, and 4) on this day all public school children were required to visit his grave, sing songs, and toss flowers upon his tomb.

McDonogh Cemetery was integrated in 1891 but in general, continues to be segregated to this day. Blacks are buried on the southern end of the site, with their feet place toward the rising sun.

GIROD STREET

Girod Street Cemetery was the first Protestant cemetery in New Orleans. Deconsecrated on January 4, 1957, it was destroyed after 135 years of existence. Before the work of demolishing the tombs and vaults could begin, the bodies had to be removed. Many of the deceased were buried in cast iron caskets, which were popular during the 1840's and 50's. Because of the glass plate, the body could be viewed after the coffin had been sealed.

The manufacturing process, involving a combination of artistic and technical expertise, consisted of several steps. A wooden mold was carved out of wood, an impression made in the sand with the mold, and molten metal poured into the impression. The caskets came in different sizes, so many different molds were required.

More than 20 tons of metal caskets were removed from the Girod Street Cemetery and sold for scrap.

IRON CASKET

CEMETERIES

SUPERDOME

There are many reasons why Girod Street Cemetery deteriorated and had to be destroyed. One of them was the erroneous idea (which was prevalent at the time) that the purchaser was to maintain their place of burial. Since the purchaser was usually in no position to take care of his own tomb, the task usually fell upon his heirs. Families die however, move away, or lose interest and the memorials become neglected and decay into oblivion.

One of the interesting features about Girod street was its yellow fever mound. Between 1817 and 1860 New Orleans had 23 yellow fever epidemics. In that period 28,192 deaths were recorded. In the cemetery there was an unoccupied space which was traditionally called the "yellow fever mound," which roughly measured 40' x 100'. In one of the great epidemics (no one is sure what year) this space was used for mass burials. When the cemetery was removed the mound was excavated to a depth of 5 feet and all remains reinterred in Hope Mausoleum.

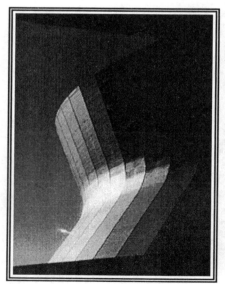

The Louisiana SUPERDOME sits on part of the old Girod Street Cemetery. Although it was never intended, this magnificent structure now serves as the largest monument in the world -- to the forgotten and neglected of the Girod Street Cemetery.

LOUISIANA
SUPERDOME

BOONDOCKS

INTRODUCTION

When you get outside the Quarter, New Orleans changes. The farther you travel from the Quarter, the more it changes. While Uptown is distinctive, Gentilly, New Orleans East, etc., are not much different from Baton Rouge, Mobile, or for that matter, any large American city. By the time one reaches Metairie, New Orleans' closest suburb, almost all traces of Creole culture has vanished. Which doesn't mean that there aren't interesting things to see. Louisiana is filled with unique places -- they just don't happen to resemble the Quarter.

Most tourists, never explore outside the Quarter. Besides the cemeteries, the New Orleans area features many worthwhile places such as City Park, the Chalmette Battlefield, and the plantation homes up and down the River. Many are accessible by streetcar, bus, taxi or ferry. Others are not and a vehicle is required. In any case, bring along your map, water, insect repellant, sunglasses, and enjoy the ride. The trip down to Lafitte for example, could possibly be the most interesting thing you've done in a long time. Another day excursion worth considering is Fort Jackson, on Hwy 23 just below Buras. During the Civil War, protection of New Orleans depended solely of Forts Jackson and St. Phillip (directly across the river from Fort Jackson). Considered impregnable and nonpassible, Fort Jackson is surrounded by a moat and at the time of the Civil War, featured 75 cannons. In April 1862 however, the Union fleet, commanded by Captain David Farragut, successfully slipped past Fort Jackson and went on to capture New Orleans. The citizens of N.O., upon hearing the news, panicked and began burning everything in sight, including most of the waterfront. After capturing New Orleans, Farragut then proceeded to negotiate the surrender of Fort Jackson. Between April 23 and the 28th over 7,500 motor shells struck the fort, which eventually surrendered.

Regarding planation homes, there are many to choose from. Probably the most impressive is Oak Alley (in Vacherie) which features an arching tunnel of live oaks 1/4 of a mile long. Somewhat closer is Destrehan Plantation, located on LA 48, on the outskirts of the New Orleans area. Records indicate that it is probably the oldest intact plantation home in the lower Mississippi Valley. Jean Lafitte supposedly buried treasure on the premises and now haunts the grounds.

BOONDOCKS

SHOTGUNS

Early Creole architecture of New Orleans can roughly be divided into 3 basic styles: 1) townhouses (upper class), 2) cottages (middle class), and 3) shotguns (lower class). Of the three, the shotguns are probably the most interesting because they are the most variable. Shotguns can contain anywhere from 2 to 8 bays (openings across the front). You can have double shotguns, two story shotguns, shotguns with galleries and porches, etc. And then you have the camelback shotguns (a one story shotgun with a two story section at the rear.)

Where did the name "shotgun" originate?

Legend has it that they were called shotguns because one could fire a gun from the front porch, through the house, and out the back door, without hitting anything in the house. Another theory is that the shotgun was developed because of the long, narrow lots that are common in New Orleans. Research however, has uncovered the fact that shotguns did not originate in New Orleans, but in the swamps, and were originally used as hunting camps, hence the name "shotgun" house.

By the way, April is officially recognized as SHOTGUN HOUSE MONTH.

1023 DUMAINE ST.

ADDRESSES

1031 Clouet -- Early shotgun.
1431 Bourbon -- Classic 2 bay, in Greek Revival.
5309 Dauphine -- Galley, iron fence, ornate woodwork.
3619 Constance --Hipped roof single shotgun with "baby" shotgun attached to side.
1477 N Robertson -- Greek Revival style 1884, used as a jazz hall.

LIBERTY MONUMENT

Probably the most controversial monument in New Orleans. It celebrated the return of "white rule" to New Orleans in 1874. Originally located at the foot of Canal Street, it was placed in storage while the street was being repaired. Three years later it was reinstalled at the foot of Iberville. Thereafter, the City Council declared the marker a "nuisance" and went to court seeking to transfer it to a museum. The matter is still pending, tied up by various law suits and court mandates.

According to one historian, during the administration of Governor Pinchback (1872), an African-American, the New Orleans Metropolitan Police, which was predominately African-American, began demanding a portion of their shakedowns in trade -- from the prostitutes of the city. Their demands so aggravated the prostitutes that they sought help from their political friends, who formed a new organization, the White League.

The Battle of Liberty Place was one of the strangest, most confusing 15 minutes in U.S. history. The White League took over the city forcing Governor Kellog into hiding (see CUSTOM HOUSE, p.21). President Grant eventually reinstated Kellog with troops but Rutherford B. Hayes later agreed to withdraw Union troops from Louisiana, effectively ending Reconstruction.

The caption at the bottom of the monument reads " A conflict of the past that should teach us a lesson for the future."

DIRECTIONS

This monument is located just outside the Quarter, near the Aquarium.

LIBERTY
MONUMENT

BOONDOCKS

STORYVILLE

Prostitution was nothing new to New Orleans before the opening of Storyville in 1897. In fact prostitutes may have been some of the first female residents of the Crescent City. In 1721 Bienville wrote to Paris, demanding women, as the men of the city were "running in the woods after Indian girls." To rectify the situation, the Mississippi Company sent 88 girls, most of whom had been inmates in a prison in Paris.

Contrary to popular belief, Storyville did not legalize prostitution. The 1897 ordinance (which was repealed in 1917) simply stated that it was unlawful for prostitutes to operate outside the given district. Another misconception deals with race. According to the ordinance, the races were to be segregated. While both black and white prostitutes were allowed to occupy the district, black women and white women were not allowed to reside in the same house.

Two of the most popular and lavish sporting houses were Lulu White's Saloon and Josie Arlington's. Lulu was an octaroon (1/8 black) from the West Indies and was considered "Queen of Storyville." Her establishment housed 5 parlors and 15 bedrooms, each with its own bath. Arlington owned a narrow Edwardian house, 4 stories tall with a cupola. Inside, one encountered a succession of parlors (Japanese, Turkish, Viennese, etc,), a hall of mirrors and elaborately furnished boudoirs. Both establishments were located on

Basin Street. Few of the original Storyville structures remain except for Frank Early's Saloon, 3 cribs, the lower story of Lulu White's, (located on Bienville between Basin and Crozat) and Big Mama's Store (on St. Louis between Treme and N. Robertson).

CORNER OF BIENVILLE & BASIN

HOLIDAY INN

On December 31, 1972 Mark Essex opened fire on the New Orleans Police Central Lockup building, killing a police cadet. Eluding police, he then hid out until January 7. Making his way up to the top of the Holiday Inn (at the time it was a Howard Johnson's), he began firing away, eventually killing 9 and seriously wounding 10 others.

Essex wasn't the only one who shot and injured people however. The police actually shot themselves. Suspecting an additional sniper on the roof, they opened fire. The bullets ricocheted however, hitting the police and injuring several of them.

Although many witnesses and police insisted there were several snipers, only Essex was shot and killed.

On the outside of the Holiday Inn, on the Uptown side, there is a gigantic, 150 foot clarinet mural, commemorating the birth-place of jazz.

DIRECTIONS

This hotel is located at 330 Loyola Avenue, 3 blocks from Canal Street.

DOWNTOWN
HOLIDAY INN

BOONDOCKS

OSWALD
4905 MAGAZINE STREET

Lee Harvey Oswald was born in New Orleans on October 18, 1939. He moved but then returned to the city during his junior high and high school years (see Exchange Alley, p.23). In 1963 he returned to the city to find a job. On April 24, upon arriving in the city, he stayed at his aunt's house, Lillian Murret, at 757 French Street. On April 26 he went to the Louisiana Dept. of Labor and told them he was a commercial photographer. The interviewer wrote down *"Will travel on limited basis, will relocate. Min. $1.25/hr. Neat. Suit. Tie. Polite."*

On May 9 he went to work at the William B. Reily Co. at 640 Magazine Street, lubricating the machinery in a coffee factory. He also rented an apartment at 4905 Magazine Street.

On July 9 he was fired by Reily.

On August 16 he began passing out *Fair Play for Cuba* literature in front of the International Trade Mart. (See Shaw p. 26)

On September 24 he left Magazine Street and boarded a bus. Two days later he was in Mexico City trying to obtain permission to enter Cuba.

4905
MAGAZINE
STREET

ANNE RICE RESIDENCE
2523 PRYTANIA

More than anything else, Anne Rice can be credited with the "feminization" of the vampire. Also, before Rice, the basic psyche of the vampire had remained largely unexamined. With Rice however, motivations and internal conflicts are examined, and he "feels" certain things. Louie, for example, in INTERVIEW, is overly concerned with his feelings and the feelings of those around him. So much so, that they oftentimes alter his behavior. In contrast, the vampire of old had little regard for his feelings, and particularly those of his victims. He simple wanted blood.

Although it appears to be an unassuming, modest chapel, this church, OUR MOTHER OF PERPETUAL HELP, is actually owned by Anne Rice. Interestingly enough, even though it is now a private structure, it continues to be used as a church, with Mass being celebrated on a regular basis. Supposedly, Anne Rice with fond memories of the chapel, approached the Redemptorists (a Roman Catholic religious order), who then sold it to Rice in April 1996. Rice's "real" residence is located at 1239 1st Street, in the Garden District. This residence also served as the setting for here fourth novel, THE WITCHING HOUR. Rice also owns several houses, incl. a former orphanage, St. Elizabeth's, (1314 Napoleon Ave) purchased in 1993, that supposedly holds her doll collection. The orphanage has also been home to the Memnoch Ball, an annual Halloween party and celebration by the Anne Rice Vampire LeStat Fan Club.

INTERVIEW WITH THE VAMPIRE spawned a major motion picture by the same name, which was partially filmed in New Orleans. In November 1993, Royal Street was covered with dirt and the filming was conducted at night. During the shoot, "minor" actors were instructed not to make eye contact with Tom Cruise.

2523 PRYTANIA

BOONDOCKS

OAKS
CITY PARK

Prior to the Civil War, practically every man in New Orleans had fought at least one duel during his lifetime. Besides St. Anthony's Square (behind the cathedral) The Oaks , now located in City Park, was the site of choice. On a single Sunday in 1837 for example, ten duels were fought under the shady trees between sunrise and noon, three of which resulted in fatalities.

Quarrels between the Creoles were never settled by fists. Instead, a strict code of dueling was employed. In French and Spanish times, the duels were usually fought with swords and ended with the first drawing of blood. When the Americans came to New Orleans, the choice of weapons broadened, with the use of firearms becoming prominent. Nevertheless, over the years, a variety of weapons were used, including axes and clubs. In 1810 for example, the opposing parties armed themselves with 8 foot sections of 3'x 3' cypress timbers and proceeded to beat each other silly. Likewise, duels were often conducted for the pettiest of reasons. One duel was fought over the size of the Mississippi River.

Old customs die hard. Although dueling was outlawed in 1839, it continued to exit, even among public officials. Even to the present it has continued to thrive. In 1953 for example, a duel was fought with automobiles at Tulane and S. Broad.

DIRECTIONS

The Oaks are located just behind the New Orleans Museum of Art.

OAKS, CITY PARK

MOUNT PLEASANT SPIRITUAL CHURCH
3423 CLOUET STREET

The origins of the Spiritual Churches of New Orleans remain obscure. They began in the 1920s as a black women's movement, influenced by Catholicism, Pentacostalism, Spiritualism and Voodoo. One of the early leaders was Mother Catherine Seals, matriarch of the Temple of Innocent Blood. After suffering a paralytic stroke, she healed herself when a white healer refused to cure her because she was black. A spirit then told her to found her own religion. She did so and began healing. According to Tallant (GUMBO YA-YA) she cured by "layin' on ob hands and anointin' dere innards with a full tumbler of warm castor oil, followed by a quarter of a lemon to kill the taste." The church building, on Charbonet Street, which she called the "Holy Manger," was by all accounts, similar to an actual manager. It contained over 500 oil lamps, which burned around the clock. During a typical sermon, parrots, canaries, and cockatoos might cry out or begin singing. Dogs would often fight over the choice spots near the heater. Donkeys, goats, hens and sheep strolled in and out of the church at their leisure. Mother Catherine always came into the church the same way, through a hole in the roof. After preaching, she would commence to healing. The lame were obliged to walk by being whipped with a wet towel and told to run. The blind were treated with rainwater, or for more resistant cases -- lightning. According to her followers, her teachings were not based on the Bible, as she was inspired by the Holy Spirit. Mother Catherine remained inside her church, without leaving the premises for 9 years. When death was imminent, she finally left her church and New Orleans and traveled to her birthplace in Kentucky. But not before telling everyone that she would be resurrected on the third day, come back, and continue her work as usual. Thousands attended the funeral, with the congregation insisting that she be buried in the Temple. The city objected however and she was buried in St. Vincent de Paul Cemetery, vault number 144, 4th tier. A large statue was placed on her grave and for many years, the faithful, both black and white, continued their daily pilgrimages.

BOONDOCKS

SWAGGERT
1131 AIRLINE HIGHWAY

According to eyewitnesses, Jimmy Swaggert visited the seedy Airline Highway strip 20-25 times, beginning in October 1986. By the time a rival preacher began spying on him and caught him in the act, Swaggert had amassed a 100 million dollar empire, which soon came crashing down.

Swaggert was defrocked April 8, 1988 as a minister of the Assembly of God for refusing to accept disciplining by church leadership. Previously, he had been ordered to stop preaching for one year in punishment for his sins.

Motels frequented by Swaggert included the Travel Inn (Room #7) at 1131 Airline Highway and the Texas Motel at 3520 Airline Highway.

Swaggert's reputation and financial support were further diminished in 1991 when on October 11, he was found in a car with a prostitute when police stopped him for a traffic violation in California. After the incident Swaggert's donations and contributions plunged by two-thirds.

As of 1996, Jimmy Swaggert Ministries is up and running again and back on the air, saving lost souls.

TRAVEL INN MOTEL

CARLOS MARCELLO
3908 CLIFFORD AVENUE, METAIRIE

Carlos Marcello was born in Tunisia and came to New Orleans as a small boy. At the age of 20 he was sent to prison for robbery. Supposedly, in 1947 he was named head of the Louisiana Mafia at a ceremony at the Black Diamond Club, on the corner of Galvez and Conti. In 1951 he was a guest of the Kefauver Committee on Organized Crime and pleaded the 5th amendment 152 times when questioned. In April 1961, on orders from Robert Kennedy, Marcello was deported to Guatemala, where he remained for two months before secretly making his way back into the United States. The government continued in its efforts to have Marcello deported again, but did not succeed. It did succeed in the BRILAB case however, in 1981. Marcello was convicted but after 6 years in prison the conviction was overturned and Marcello returned home. He died in March 1993 at the age of 83.

Various parties have linked Marcello to the Kennedy assassination, supposedly in revenge for his deportation. Others said he was one of the most powerful men in the country. On the other hand, when the New Orleans office of the FBI investigated him, they reported he was a "stupid little man" who could not possibly be involved in anything and appeared to be exactly what he said he was -- a salesman for the Pelican Tomato Company.

LOCATIONS
--1908 Clifford Dr, Metairie (former residence).
--Pelican Tomato Company, 4905 Kent Ave., Metairie.
--1525 Airline Hwy. Currently, Lucky Coin Machine. Previously the Town and Country Motel, the headquarters of the Marcello business interests.

1908 CLIFFORD DRIVE

BOONDOCKS

LAFITTE CEMETERY
LAFITTE, LA.

According to one legend Jean Lafitte is buried in a small cemetery in Lafitte, LA , along with Napoleon and John Paul Jones.

On Feb. 28, 1819, at 7:30 p.m. Napoleon Bonaparte, while sitting on the shores of St. Helena, felt a tug at his sleeve. It was his cousin, Jean Lafitte. Substituting a look-alike double for himself, Napoleon and Jean waded to a pirogue (small boat) then rowed 15 miles to a schooner. From there, they headed for New Orleans, to establish a new French empire (with the Napoleon House to be his official residence). In the meantime, serving as a decoy, the SERAPHINE sailed out of New Orleans to confuse officials. Near the Yucatan, Napoleon had a heart attack or stroke and died. From there he was taken to Lafitte Cemetery, which was owned by Jean Lafitte. (Napoleon's double, back on St. Helena, was poisoned in 1821. The death mask Napoleon's doctor brought with him on his visit to New Orleans was not cast from the real Napoleon, but from his double.)

Wounded during a sea battle, Lafitte died in the 1830's. His sailors took his body to the same cemetery and buried him there in 1839 next to Napoleon. Years later, someone placed the iron cross upon his grave.

NAPOLEON HOUSE

John Paul Jones, Lafitte's uncle, died in Brittany in 1789 and was buried there. Some time later his body was exhumed and returned to the U.S. Naval Academy. Somehow they got the wrong body. A year later, Jean Lafitte, (12 years old at the time), arrived and took the real body back to Lafitte Cemetery.

LAFITTE CEMETERY
LAFITTE, LA. (continued)

DIRECTIONS

Take the CCC over the Mississippi River to the Westbank. Stay in the center lane. This will put you on the Westbank Expressway. Take the WBX to the Barataria Blvd. exit. Take a left on Hwy 45 South. Go 2.8 miles. Take a left on LA 3134. Go 7.2 miles (cross over the Intracoastal bridge) until you reach the intersection of LA 303 and Hwy 45 South. Take a left and go 6.7 miles until you reach Goose Bayou bridge. Take an immediate right after you cross the bridge at the Turgeon Tours sign. The cemetery is located at the edge of the water.

LAGNIAPPE

Other attractions in the area include the Jean Lafitte National Park Visitor's Center (near Crown Point) and the Berthoud Cemetery (on a gravel road, 2.5 miles from the intersection of LA 303 and Hwy 45 S) which is situated on top of an Indian mound.

LAFITTE CEMETERY

BOONDOCKS

BATTLE OF NEW ORLEANS
CHALMETTE BATTLEFIELD

The Battle of New Orleans was one of the most lopsided in history. Most of the casualties occurred within a thirty minute rout, mowed down by the American forces who had positioned themselves behind an earthen wall and cotton bales. Estimates of British casualties vary greatly. Their own reports listed over 2,000 killed, wounded and missing. The official American estimate was 2,600. On the American side losses were listed as 7 killed and 6 wounded. The most amazing thing about the battle was that it was fought 15 days after the peace treaty had been signed and theoretically, had no military significance. Many historians contend however that the battle was very significant. They argue that if the U.S. would have lost, England would have negated the treaty and continued the war. Other historians disagree. They maintain both sides were tired of war, anxious to get it over, and ready for peace. According to this theory, the wording of the treaty clearly indicated that England was not interested in defeating the U.S. nor acquiring more territory. The real reason England wanted peace was because they were afraid of suffering further naval defeats and losing Canada.

Which view is correct? Was Britain eager for peace or more territory? Well -- pretend you are in charge of the British forces. You are aware you have approx. 8,000 well-trained troops some-where in the vicinity of Louisiana. They are either on the way, have arrived, or have already left. As far as you know, your

troops may have already won a complete victory. If you were dead serious about bringing the U.S. to its knees and acquiring new territory, would you sign a treaty or wait a few days?

CHALMETTE
BATTLEFIELD

BATTLE OF NEW ORLEANS
CHALMETTE BATTLEFIELD

Chalmette Battlefield and Chalmette National Cemetery lie down river from New Orleans, about 5 miles from the French Quarter. Chalmette Monument, a 100 foot obelisk, marks the site of Jackson's position during the Battle of New Orleans. This monument, which was begun in 1840, was not completed until 1908, 68 years after the cornerstone was laid. Although Jackson subsequently became a hero and later President largely because of his heroic actions at this site, many New Orleanians were overjoyed at his departure from the city.

Two days after the battle, Jackson continued to impose martial law, fearing the return of the British troops. Militia companies, which had looked forward to disbandment, were again marched into camps and set to drilling. Throughout the city there was grumbling, talk of mutiny, and a general feeling of dissatisfaction with Jackson. In the meantime, French citizens (all of Louisiana was French until 1803) in the militia discovered that they could obtain a discharge by registering their nationality at the French consulate. Jackson matched this trick with one of his own by deporting the holders of such papers to Baton Rouge (about 100 miles away). The remaining French subjects sympathized with their exiled compatriots and the Louisiana troops at Chef Mentuer mutinied.

DIRECTIONS

The Battlefield can be reached several ways, including by steamboat. If you are on the Westbank however, take the Chalmette ferry.

CHALMETTE MONUMENT

BOONDOCKS

BATTLE OF NEW ORLEANS
ANDREW JACKSON

LA COURRIERE DE LA LOUISIANE, a French newspaper, published a lengthy communication criticizing Jackson (see p.63). Jackson demanded the name of the author, discovered his whereabouts, and Louis Louaillier was arrested on Sunday, March 5. A Creole lawyer offered his services to Louaillier on the spot. He sped to the residence of Federal Judge Hall with a petition for a writ of habeas corpus, which was granted. Jackson then promptly arrested Judge Hall "for abiding, abetting, and exciting mutiny within my camp."

Judge Hall soon took his revenge however. The peace treaty was signed and martial law lifted. All prisoners were released, including Hall and Louaillier. On March 21 Hall issued a summons directing Jackson to show cause why he should not be held in contempt for refusal to recognize the writ of habeas corpus in the Louaillier case. He ordered the defendant to appear and receive the sentence of the court.

The trial (which took place at 919 Royal Street) was short and to the point. Jackson declined to respond to the interrogations of the District Attorney and this left the Court "with no alternative." A fine of $1000 and costs were imposed on Jackson.

Afterward, an attempt was made by a certain few (Lafitte's cronies) to raise the amount of the General's fine by public subscription. After raising only $160, the scheme was abandoned and the money donated to the poor.

ANDREW JACKSON HOTEL, 919 ROYAL ST.

CHALMETTE BATTLEFIELD
BUFFALO BILL

Each year on the anniversary of the Battle of New Orleans a reenactment is held, complete with cannon fire, marching soldiers, and authentic displays. Perhaps the most memorable reenactment occurred in 1885, in Oakland Park.

In the winter of 1884-85, during the first New Orleans World Expo, Buffalo Bill Cody's Wild West Show hit the city with high expectations. Forty-four days of rain dampened things a bit but the show went on. On Feb. 1, Cody made good on his promise of a special showing for the citizens of N.O. Following a spectacular fireworks display, Cody's drama company presented a dramatization of the Battle of New Orleans.

As expected, Cody played the part of Gen. Jackson. If not for anyone else, it was an extremely significant event -- an acting debut of sorts. It was the only time in his career that Cody portrayed anyone other than himself.

The colorful cast, with no script or historical records to go by, ad-libbed the show, thereby making its authenticity doubtful. In any event, it probably didn't matter. Smoke from the rifles and fireworks covered the entire stage, making it difficult, if not impossible to see the show.

REENACTMENT,
BATTLE OF NEW
ORLEANS

BOONDOCKS

CHALMETTE CEMETERY

There are many misconceptions concerning Chalmette National Cemetery. Popular belief has it that this cemetery holds the bodies of those killed in the Battle of New Orleans. Others, who consider themselves more knowledgeable, believe that it was established for Confederate troops killed in the Civil War. Others contend that the cemetery was closed in 1945.

The facts are:
1) Chalmette Cemetery was created for the interment of Union soldiers killed in the Civil War.
2) The first soldiers, who were black, were buried on May 5, 1864.
3) Casualties from all wars, with the exception of the Revolutionary and Korean Wars, are represented in the cemetery, including Vietnam.

If one tires of walking around the cemetery, he can head for the Superintendent's House. There he can inspect the American flag, read the Gettysburg address, and look over a copy of the Declaration of Independence. These items are always on display, as they are in every national cemetery in the country. Incidently, the Gettysburg Address was not written by Lincoln on the back of an envelope while he was on the train. It was written in Washington, before he left. There are 5 versions of the speech, all different. The 5th version is the one carved in the Lincoln Memorial.

CHALMETTE CEMETERY

CHALMETTE CEMETERY

For most Americans, Vietnam was our first military defeat. But the facts speak differently.

In the Civil War, 1,000,000 men were killed or wounded. Deaths totaled 529,332. The North lost 364,511 men, the South half as many, 164,821. Disease killed more men than bullets. About 140,000 Union troops and 75,000 Confederates died in battle.

Chalmette is primarily a Civil War Cemetery. Of the 15,000 veterans buried on the 7 ½ acres, only 6,700 have names. The rest have numbers.

Of the 2,000 British troops that died on the Battlefield during the Battle of New Orleans, nothing is known of their whereabouts. They have no names or numbers. Presumably, they are buried somewhere on or near the battlefield, but no one is sure.

MARKER #9413,
CHALMETTE CEMETERY

MUSIC & LITERATURE

INTRODUCTION

Over the years, New Orleans has been blessed with an abundance of talented artists and writers, both homegrown and imported. Although New Orleans is known for jazz, it is also famous for other forms of music, such as gospel, Cajun, rock and rhythm & blues.

For some reason, writers love New Orleans, even to this day. The curious thing is that most never stay for very long -- a year or two at the most. The list is long, beginning with Walt Whitman, who lived in the city for three months in 1848 while working for a newspaper, THE DAILY CRESCENT.

OTHER WRITERS:

*Thornton Wilder -- rented apartment at 623 Bourbon.
*Sherwood Anderson -- lived all over the city. In January 1922 he lived in a 3rd floor apartment at 708 Royal. In 1925 he lived at 540B St. Peter and 825 Bourbon. From 1925-1927 he lived at 715 Gov. Nicholls. Writing Gertrude Stein, he said he was living in "the most civilized place I have ever found in America." Anderson also lived in the Pontalba Apartments shortly after the publication of WINESBURG, OHIO.
*O. Henry -- a frequent patron at Madame Begue's Restaurant at 823 Decatur (now Tujaque's).
*John Dos Passos -- lived at 510 Esplanade during February and March 1923, while working on MANHATTAN TRANSFER. According to Passos, New Orleans was "full of noise and jingle, horseracing, crap shooting, whoring, and bawdry."
*Sinclair Lewis -- winner of the Nobel Prize in Literature (1930), lived at 1536 Nashville during the 1920's.
*Walker Percy -- author of the MOVIEGOER, LOVE IN THE RUINS, the THANATOS SYNDROME, etc., resided at 1820 Milan in 1958.
*William Faulkner -- lived at 624 Pirate's Alley (now the Faulkner House). When Faulkner moved in, the only thing he owned was a tea kettle.
*F. Scott Fitzgerald -- associated with 2900 Prytania.

SOUTH RAMPART & PERDIDO

This is truly one of the most historic locations in New Orleans, for several reasons. Anyone interested in jazz should venture here, genuflect, and say a few prayers to their favorite saint.

This is the spot where, as a small boy, little Louie Armstrong was arrested for firing a gun into the air, which subsequently led to his incarceration in the Waif's Home, where he learned to play several instruments. Before this incident, Armstrong was a small boy without direction or opportunity, and probably would have ended up singing and dancing on street corners for the rest of his life, or worse.

Armstrong is also associated with this corner for another reason. Jake Itzkowitz had a pawn store here on the first floor and it is very likely that this is the place where Armstrong bought his first cornet.

The first floor also housed a saloon known as the "Eagle," which was frequented by jazz musicians. The third floor of the same building housed the Odd Fellows Association. Musicians of all kinds played here, including Buddy Bolden and other early jazz musicians. In fact, all along S. Rampart, towards Uptown, early jazz clubs lined the street. A few of the original buildings are still intact.

S. RAMPART & PERDIDO

MUSIC & LITERATURE

BUDDY BOLDEN
2309 FIRST STREET

Buddy Bolden was the first important figure in the birth of jazz. According to some, he invented the art form. Although no recordings exist of his music, he was a major influence on most of the early jazz musicians in N.O. He played the cornet with such force that his music often carried miles in the thick, hot air of the summer nights. When his band paraded, Buddy had three women at his side, one to carry his cornet, one his coat, and one his hat.

Although a legendary figure, he died in obscurity. Spending the last 24 years of his life in an insane asylum, he passed away in 1931. Bolden was buried in Holt Cemetery, where many of the city's indigent were put to rest, in plot C-623. For lack of payment, after two years his remains were dug up, reburied deeper, and another burial made on top. Plot C-623 was subsequently changed and no records kept of the original burial spot.

On Sept 6, 1996, Bolden finally got his due. A jazz funeral was held in his honor and a marker placed in the cemetery. Even though the funeral was 65 years late and the marker was not placed over the exact site of his burial, no one seemed to mind.

Places Bolden played (according to Bunk Johnson, who played with Bolden) that are still standing:

-- 907 St. Claude, Masonic Dance Hall.
-- Odd Fellows Hall, 628 Seguin (Algiers).
-- Economy Hall, 1422 Ursaline.
-- Perseverance Hall, 1644 N. Villere Street (now a Spiritual Church).

2309 FIRST STREET

FATS DOMINO
5525 MARAIS

Between 1955 and 1963, Fats Domino had 37 Top 40 hits, and was probably the most famous rhythm & blues artist in the world.

Fats, whose real name is Antoine was born in New Orleans on February 28, 1928. His first recording, the Fat Man, was a million seller. Since the 1970s however, he has played sporadically but still performs, in such venues as Las Vegas.

Fats was inducted into the Rock and Roll Hall of Fame in 1986. Curiously enough however, he never had a Number 1 hit. His biggest hit, Blueberry Hill, only went to #2, but stayed in the top 40 for 21 weeks.

His residence is located on Marais, one block off St. Claude. The house is surrounded by a white fence. The decorative flowers in the fence are painted pink and yellow. The same pink and yellow colors have been employed on the exterior trim of the house. The front yard contains a huge satellite dish, and the house is surrounded by obvious surveillance cameras. On top the roof 20-25 pigeons usually sit, as if waiting for someone to come out and feed them. Next door, at 1208 Caffin, sits Fats Domino Publishing.

1208
CAFFIN
AVENUE

MUSIC & LITERATURE

LITTLE RICHARD
838 N. RAMPART

Unquestionably, one of the fathers of rock & roll, Little Richard was born Richard Wayne Penniman on December 5, 1932 in Macon, Georgia. Many of his early hits were recorded in New Orleans at J & M Studio, located at 838 N. Rampart (corner of N. Rampart and Dumaine). At the time the studio was located in the back of a furniture store. According to Little Richard, there was no overdubbing. Each recording was done over and over again, sometimes 60 or 70 times, until it was right. Tutti-Frutti however, which was recorded on September 14, 1955 was done in three takes, using Fats Domino's session men. Other recordings at this studio included Ready Teddy on May 10, 1956 and Good Golly Miss Molly, recorded on Oct 16, 1956.

In 1957, at the height of his popularity, during the middle of a tour of Australia, Little Richard announced he was quitting rock & roll forever. Leaving behind half a million dollars worth of canceled bookings and several lawsuits, he told his band he was going to devote his life to God. By the time he got back to the U.S. the story was big news, with rumors running rampant concerning the reason for his retirement. Nevertheless, true to his word, he began playing and recording religious and gospel music until 1964, when he recorded Whole Lotta Shakin' and Lawdy Miss Clawdy.

838 N. RAMPART

The original site, 828 N. Rampart, was an appliance store owned by Cosimo "Coz" Matassa. Later Coz began selling records and eventually created a recording studio in the back room. Later he moved the studio to 523 Gov. Nicholls, then 525 Gov. Nicholls, then 748 Camp St. (which is currently a steak house/ rock & roll museum).

MUSIC & LITERATURE

JELLY ROLL MORTON
1442 FRENCHMAN

Born at the corner of Frenchman and N. Robertson in 1890 in New Orleans, Jelly Roll Morton (Ferdinand LaMenthe) began playing piano at the age of 10 and began working in the bordellos of Storyville at the age of 12. Before long his grandparents (who were raising him) found out about his trips to Storyville and kicked him out of the house at the age of 15. Soon, Jelly Roll became a favorite of the club owners (and the ladies) and began earning over $100 a night playing the piano in such places at Hilma Burt's mansion on Basin Street. By the 1930's however, Morton's style was seen as old-fashioned and he drifted into obscurity. In 1938 Alan Lomax (who also recorded Leadbelly) recorded Jelly Roll in a series of interviews held at the Library of Congress. His words and music helped to rekindle an interest in Morton, which eventually led to further recording dates and a renewed career, which was cut short by illness and death in Los Angeles in 1941.

According to most scholars, LaMenthe ranks as one of the great composers of jazz, in the same league with Duke Ellington, Thelonius Monk and Charlie Mingus. As can be expected, Jelly Roll had a lot to say about jazz, the origins of jazz and how it should be played. Perhaps his most noted statement was that he actually invented jazz in 1902 (when he was 17 years old), supposedly at a club called the Frenchman's on the corner of Villere and Bienville. He also said that the "Spanish tinge" he placed in his music was responsible for it being

different from ragtime and other music at the time. With regard to composing, he claimed he was merely trying to imitate an entire band, by creating rhythm, harmony and melody all at the same time on the piano.

Jelly Roll is as popular today as he ever was. Probably more so. Likewise, his recordings are collector's items, going for as much as $500 per record.

1442 FRENCHMAN

73

MUSIC & LITERATURE

HANK WILLIAMS
MUNICIPAL AUDITORIUM

In many ways, Hank Williams was the forerunner of Elvis Presley. Both had their roots in country blues, both were superstars, both changed the face of popular music, and both suffered the same problems, with regard to drugs. The main difference is that a lot of people knew about Hank's problems from Day 1. Early on they put up with it but later, as his conditioned deteriorated, they couldn't close their eyes to the problem. Williams, a Grand Ole Opry star, was finally kicked off the stage, left Nashville, and ventured back to Louisiana, to the Louisiana Hayride (another corollary with Elvis).

Within the space of two days, Hank Williams was married three times -- to the same woman. On Saturday, October 18, 1952, Hank and Billie Jean Jones drove to Minden, Louisiana, where they were married by a Justice of the Peace. Hank then married Billie Jean in a public marriage in New Orleans on Sunday, October 19. Tickets ranged from $1 to $2.80. 14,000 people witnessed the spectacle in the Municipal Auditorium at 3 o'clock and again at 7 o'clock. Williams, drunk the whole day, finally passed out at the Jung Hotel.

Two months later, on January 1, 1953, Hank Williams died.

TIPS

The Municipal Auditorium, which was converted into a casino in 1993, is scheduled to be restored back to its original condition by May 1997.

MUNICIPAL AUDITORIUM, ARMSTRONG PARK

MUSIC & LITERATURE

GRAM PARSONS
GARDEN OF MEMORIES

Gram Parsons, a member of the Byrds and Flying Burrito Brothers, was one of the early pioneers of "country-rock."

Parsons died in Joshua Tree, a wilderness area 2 hours east of Los Angeles. Bob Parsons, his stepfather and a N.O. native, began the funeral arrangements in New Orleans.

Gram however, had told friends that he wanted to be cremated, with his ashes spread over Joshua Tree. Friends, including Phil Kaufman, found out which airline was due to ship the body, borrowed a hearse, took the coffin, and carried it out to Cap Rock in Joshua Tree. Opening the casket, Kaufman poured gasoline on the body and set it on fire, where it was spotted the next day.

The remains were shipped to New Orleans. Phil Kaufman was arrested for stealing the coffin and charged with grand theft.

On Sept 25, 1973 he was buried in Garden of Memories, 4800 Airline Highway. The inscription, on a saucer-sized plaque, reads "God's own singer." The burial spot , in Section R, about 10 rows from the road, is marked by a small metal sign.

GRAM PARSONS' BURIAL PLOT

MUSIC & LITERATURE

TENNESSEE WILLIAMS
722 TOULOUSE

Although Williams was not born in New Orleans, he claimed he felt most at home here and occupied many residences in the Crescent City throughout his life.

His short stay at 722 Toulouse was probably his most memorable. One night, the landlady was so angered by a wild party on the ground floor that she poured boiling water through the floorboards. The police were called and she was charged with "malicious mischief," and fined $15. Reluctantly, TW had to testify at the hearing. TW's rent at this address was $10/month. He lived on the third floor, the room with the gabled window.

Williams also lived at 431 Royal, 708 Toulouse (Sept 1941), 538 Royal (Oct 1941), had an apartment at 632 St. Peter, and a residence at 1014 Dumaine.

On March 31, 1996 during the Tennessee Williams Literary Festival, a Stella and Stanley shouting contest was held for the first time. Contestants were required to mimic Stanley Kowalski's famous "Stella !!!" line, (from A STREETCAR NAMED DESIRE). The "Stanleys" stood on the ground, shouting up to "Stella" on the balcony at the corner of St. Peter and Decatur.

722 TOULOUSE

MUSIC & LITERATURE

WILLIAM BURROUGHS
509 WAGNER, ALGIERS

A graduate of Harvard in 1936, Burroughs studied medicine in Vienna, worked as a detective, bartender and pest exterminator. He also cut off one of his fingers during a "Van Gogh kick." Eventually, as seen in ON THE ROAD, he became a heroin addict, killed his wife while shooting an apple off her head and wrote NAKED LUNCH. During 1949 he lived at 509 Wagner St. in Algiers and was visited there by Jack Kerouac and friends, as depicted in ON THE ROAD. On August 17, 1996 a commemorative plaque was placed on the house.

Kerouac wrote ON THE ROAD in 3 weeks during April 1951. It was typed as one, long paragraph on a single roll of paper 120 feet long. It wasn't published however until Sept. 1957.

For the rest of his life Kerouac insisted the characters in ON THE ROAD were on a spiritual quest, but no one seemed to take this view seriously. Kerouac died in 1968. Jan, his only child, died on June 7, 1996.

LOCATION

From the French Quarter, the best way to reach the house is by the Canal Street ferry. It may take longer, but you probably won't get lost. The way back is even easier. At the end of Wagner, simply take a left on River Road and follow it all the way back to the ferry.

509 WAGNER, ALGIERS

MUSIC & LITERATURE

TRUMAN CAPOTE
MONTELEONE HOTEL

Capote was born in Touro Infirmary on Sept. 30, 1924. For a short time after his birth his family lived at the Monteleone Hotel (214 Royal Street).

Capote was known for his quick wit and whining voice, as well as his literary accomplishments, such as IN COLD BLOOD. He was also known for his flamboyant lifestyle, including his use of drugs and alcohol. In August 1983 for example, he was lambasted by a judge for appearing in court wearing Bermuda shorts during a DWI hearing.

Capote spent most of his life in New York but occasionally drifted back to New Orleans several times during his career. In 1945 (for example) he lived in an apartment at 711 Royal Street.

One story about Capote stands above the rest. While vacationing in Key West he was approached by a woman who wanted an autograph. When Truman agreed, she promptly pulled down her underwear and bent over. Capote was then immediately approached by a man, who wanted the same, but on his penis. Capote looked down, sized up the situation, and promptly replied that an autograph was out of the question. However, he might be able to initial it.

MONTELEONE
HOTEL

78

MUSIC & LITERATURE

JOHN KENNEDY TOOLE
1016 ELYSIAN FIELDS

John Kennedy Toole, author of the Pulitzer Prize novel, A CONFEDERACY OF DUNCES, was born in 1937. It is widely believed that Toole committed suicide because he could not get his novel published. This is probably not true. Six months before his suicide his colleagues noticed a change in his personality, a developing paranoia. He told one of his friends he was hearing voices and that people were spying on him. In January 1969 he simply took off and disappeared without contacting his family. Apparently, he began driving around the country, visiting places like the Hearst mansion in San Simeon. On March 26, 1969 Toole drove to a secluded beach near Biloxi Mississippi, ran a hose from his exhaust pipe to the inside of his car and locked himself inside. He left a suicide note but his mother destroyed it after reading it and refused to divulge its contents.

When John was born the family was living at 1128 Webster. They lived at 390 Audubon when John arrived back from the service. Thelma, his mother was living at 1016 Elysian Fields when she died. Her will stipulated that 1016 Elysian Fields was to be converted into a museum for her son (it wasn't) and that NEON BIBLE, Toole's first novel, was never to be published (it was).

1016 ELYSIAN FIELDS

ETC.

INTRODUCTION

New Orleans has always been known for its diverse culture and laissez faire attitude toward alternative lifestyles and beliefs. Probably nowhere else in the U.S. does this hold true as it does in New Orleans -- which is puzzling. On the one hand New Orleans is rather conservative, part of the deep South. On the other hand, it has Mardi Gras, gambling, Bourbon Street, and formerly Storyville, Gallatin Street and the Louisiana Lottery. Seemingly, as long as the activities have been confined to certain areas, New Orleanians have been willing to turn their heads to "live and let live."

*BOTANICAS (supply religious goods, candles and herbs for voodoo and Santeria practitioners.)
   -- F& F Botanica, 801 N Broad
   -- Island of Salvation Botanica, 835 Piety St.

*PSYCHIC
   -- Hauntings Ghost Expeditions -- 635 Toulouse. Daily tours offered to visit sites of present day ghosts.

*VOODOO
   -- New Orleans Historic Voodoo Museum, 724 Dumaine St.
   -- Voodoo Spiritual Temple -- 828 N Rampart -- Services include consultations (African bone readings), rituals (voodoo weddings and snake dance rituals), and potions (juju for protection and mojo for success). The Temple also has its own home page on the World Wide Web.

*NECROMACY (a form of magic which employs rituals (often involving corpses) for the purpose of achieving various spiritual and physical states)
   -- Siren Song -- The Goddess' Boudoir -- 5221 Magazine #1. Art gallery, museum, bookstore.

INTRODUCTION (continued)

*GAY
-- Wolfendale's, 834 N Rampart. Black gay nightclub, features the Rampart Revue on Thursday nights.
-- Oz, 800 Bourbon. Features Thursday night Calendar Boy revue.
-- T. T.'s Club, 820 N. Rampart. Features T. T. Thompson, female impersonator.
-- Second Skin Leather, 521 St. Phillip.
-- The Mint, 504 Esplanade. Cabaret atmosphere.

*WITCHCRAFT
-- Witches Closet, 521 St. Phillip. Owned by certified witches. Hexes removed.

*ENVIRONMENTAL
-- Hempstead Company Store -- 607 Chartres St. Supplier of hemp and hemp related products.

*GENERATION X
--Dungeon -- 738 Toulouse. Hard core grunge. Opens at midnight.

828 N. RAMPART

ETC.

MARDI GRAS

SHORT HISTORY OF MARDI GRAS MAYHEM

1837 --- 1st public parade.

1854 --- Roving bands of pranksters pelt onlookers with bags of flour, dust, and quicklime, prompting the BEE (NO newspaper) to call for an end to Mardi Gras, as it "had become vulgar, tasteless, and spiritless."

1857---First torch-lit parade by Comus, employing the still controversial "flambeaux" carriers.

1860s -- Civil War interrupts festivities.

1873 --- Political unrest hinders Mardi Gras. Comus parade blocked by an irate crowd on Canal Street and forced to turn around and retreat.

1879 --- Mardi Gras canceled (except for Rex) because of yellow fever epidemic.

1890 --- Comus and Proteus parades meet on Canal Street at same time, with both refusing to yield to the other.

1899 --- Temperature falls to 7 degrees F. Rex parades with frozen mustache.

1949 --- Louis Armstrong reigns as King Zulu.

1950s -- Mules abandoned, first tractors used to pull floats.

1960s -- Tourist Commission tries to discourage "hippies" from attending the 'World's Greatest Free Show."

1961 -- Zulu parade almost canceled by protesting blacks, who claim makeup and costumes are undignified.

1970 -- Trumpeter Al Hirt hit by brick while riding in parade.

1979 -- Police strike cancels 13 parades. 12 others move to suburbs.

1992 -- N.O. city ordinance requires all parading crews to open membership to women, men and minorities. Comus, Momus, and Proteus cancel their parades. Rex opens membership.

TIPS

Motorists involved in traffic accidents in New Orleans during Mardi Gras should not expect the police to show up unless they hit a bus, block a parade route, are drunk, or live out of state.

ZULU

Undoubtedly, the most popular parade on Fat Tuesday is Zulu, which usually begins at 8:00 a.m.. Formerly, Zulu did not have an established route and might end up anywhere. Today however, it is more conventional and sticks to the designated streets. Zulu, also has a ball the previous weekend, and various parties leading up to Mardi Gras, such as the Witch Doctor's Party and the Big Shot's party. While a few of the treasured coconuts are given out during the parade, they are hard to come by -- unless you know someone. Zulu does have a shop however, at 722 N. Broad Street, next to the club, that sells collectibles, if one is desperate.

More people come to New Orleans during Carnival season (which runs from Jan. 6 through Fat Tuesday) than any other time. Accordingly, to obtain accommodations, one must book reservations a year in advance or more. To get the most out of Carnival, one needs a guide, of which there are many. Local papers also carry a list of activities, including the neighboring parishes, such as Jefferson and St. Bernard. Although the guides tell you a lot, they don't mention everything because there is so much to mention. Besides the parades, there are balls and other affairs, which are private and require tickets and invitations. To attend, you have to have connections.

Getting around on Fat Tuesday is almost impossible. The parades begin early and a lot of streets are blocked off, so buses, taxis and streetcars are no good. The best way to get around is to walk, or get where you are going early (before 6 a.m.). Driving in from out of town on Fat Tuesday is suicidal. If you do attempt it however, your best bet is to drive over the CCC to the Westbank, park around the Catholic church (about 5 blocks from the river) and take the ferry over to the French Quarter.

KING ZULU, 1997

ETC.

MARDI GRAS INDIANS

The origins of the Mardi Gras Indians are just as obscure as the origins of the Spiritual churches. Which is only fitting. After all, what could be more obscure than gangs of African Americans dressing up like Indians and dancing around on Fat Tuesday? It seems likely however that they originated over 100 years ago, shortly after the Buffalo Bill Wild West Show visited New Orleans in 1885. The Cotton Exposition, also in 1885, also featured Indians parading around, especially around Mardi Gras. Since blacks were not allowed the same opportunities and privileges as whites, the blacks solved the problem by forsaking their "blackness" and becoming "indians," if only for one day a year. Whatever the origins, the groups are well organized into various tribes. When the tribes meet out on the street, they fall into a type of ritualized battle, by dancing, beating drums, singing, and displaying their "colors" to each other. In past years, the battles oftentimes became bloody and violent. Nowadays however, it's more respectable, with the "big chiefs" often exchanging pleasantries and chit chat.

The costumes are elaborate, consisting of beadwork, feathers, and complex designs. The Indians, who make the costumes themselves, often spend an entire year on the task. The costumes may cost thousands of dollars and weigh more than 100 pounds.

You can catch the Indians on Mardi Gras day at various places, as they parade all day, but there is no set route on Mardi Gras. The best bet is at the corner of Orleans and Claiborne Avenues. On the Sunday before St. Joseph's Day however, there is a parade with a set route and time, although this too may vary depending on the whims of the participants.

MARDI GRAS INDIAN

JAZZ FUNERALS

Music accompanies every significant aspect of life for the average New Orleanian. Death and funerals are no exception. Today, jazz funerals are rare and given only for former practitioners of the art, such as KoKoMoJo. KoKo entertained French Quarter revelers with an assortment of instruments, including tin cans, a kazoo, and a make believe microphone made from a Christmas tree stand.

In its infancy, jazz was not respected, even by many musicians. In fact, it was looked down upon. It certainly wasn't the kind of music one played at funerals. Most brass bands of the late 1800's played marching music, ballads, and traditional favorites. In his early career, Louis Armstrong played in one of these bands. On the way to the cemetery, these bands played slow, respectable, and even solemn music. Nothing fancy. On their way home however, things changed. The musicians were on their own, no longer on the payroll. To counteract the glumness of the funeral, and to make themselves feel better, the tempo of the music was picked up. Jazz (the rap music of the early 1900's) came blaring out by one or two members, and was picked up by the others. Jazz was not created by these bands. It was already around, in the streets, here and there. The brass bands simply helped bring it out into the open.

Eventually, jazz became respectable, not only in the honky-tonks but everywhere. Soon, this new music was incorporated into the funeral procession, and over the years everyone grew to expect it, and even demand it.

KOKOMOJO
JAZZ FUNERAL,
CANAL STREET

ETC.

CAST IRON

One of the most noticeable aspects of New Orleans architecture, especially in the French Quarter, is the prevalence of iron balconies. Contrary to popular belief, most of this work is not wrought iron but cast iron, fashioned by pouring molten iron into molds. The fence around Jackson Square for example, is cast iron. Typically, any ironwork that displays an intricate pattern is also cast iron. Wrought iron, which is stronger, is usually used in doorways and gates. The gate at Lafayette I is fashioned from wrought iron, while the fence surrounding the cemetery consists of cast iron.

Incidently, one of the most famous landmarks in New Orleans happens to be a fence -- the Cornstalk Fence at 915 Royal. It too, is cast iron.

CAST IRON, DETAIL

TIPS

Royal Street, in the French Quarter, is famous for its iron balconies.

OUR LADY OF GUADALUPE
411 NORTH RAMPART

Our Lady of Guadalupe Chapel is also called the Mortuary Chapel. Recognized as the oldest chapel in New Orleans, it was founded in 1826 during the yellow fever epidemic. No one wanted to hold services for the yellow fever victims in the main church, so they built a chapel near the cemeteries.

The chapel is also home to the Shrine of St. Jude, the patron saint of lost causes. It also houses a statue of St. Expedite. Supposedly, this saint was created by unknown parishioners who, seeing only the word "expedite" on the shipping crate, mistook it for his name.

OUR LADY OF GUADALUPE

ST. EXPEDITE

LAGNIAPPE

In the last century the source of yellow fever was a mystery. Many believed it was due to swamp gas. To counteract the gas, fires were often set. Surprisingly, it sometimes worked, but not for the reason it was believed.

"MUST DO" LIST

If you only have one day to do New Orleans, some things should not be missed. The following itinerary is recommended.

8:00 - 8:30 a.m. -- **CAFE DU MONDE.** Beignets and café au lait. After breakfast slip down to the Moonwalk for a panoramic view of the River.

8:30 - 10:30 a.m. -- **CABILDO.** Take a couple of hours to get a historic perspective on the city and Louisiana.

10:30 - 12 noon. -- Walk up Orleans Avenue, take a left on Rampart, go uptown a few blocks and take a right to Basin and **ST. LOUIS I CEMETERY.** Do not go alone.

12 - 12:30 -- Go back into the Quarter toward the River to the **CENTRAL GROCERY** on Decatur Street. Order a muffuletta for lunch.

12:30 - 2 p.m. -- **OLD U. S. MINT** on Esplanade. Spend an hour or so at the Jazz Museum. Pass through the Mardi Gras exhibit. Check out the bookstore and gift shop as you leave.

2 - 3 p.m. -- Catch the streetcar that runs along the River. Take it back to the Iberville Street- Bienville Street area. Go to the **NAPOLEON HOUSE** for a cool drink. Sit back and watch the tourists.

3- 5 p.m. -- Catch the streetcar on Canal Street. Take it uptown. The entire round trip (back to Canal) runs about 2 ½ hours. You should get off however at **RIVERBEND** for dinner. (Camellia Grill, for example). Afterwards, take the streetcar back to the Quarter.

5- 6 p.m.-- If you are still hungry you might try the **ACME OYSTER HOUSE** or **FELIX'S** (both on Iberville) for some salty raw oysters.

6 p.m. - 'til. -- Cap off the evening at **LAFITTE'S BLACKSMITH SHOP** on Bourbon. The atmosphere is unique. If you want to do the tourist thing, walk down Bourbon Street on your way home.

SELECTED BIBLIOGRAPHY

Asbury, Herbert. *The French Quarter: an informal history of the New Orleans underworld.* Atlanta: Mockingbird Books, 1976.

Christovich, Mary Louise. *New Orleans Architecture, vol. 3: The Cemeteries.* Gretna, La: Pelican Publishing, 1974.

Davis, John H. *Mafia Kingfish: Carlos Marcello and the assassination of John F. Kennedy.* New York: McGraw-Hill, 1988.

Federal Writers Project, New Orleans. *New Orleans City Guide.* Boston: Houghton Mifflin, 1938.

Fong-Torres, Ben. *Hickory Wind: the life and times of Gram Parsons.* New York: Pocket Books, 1991.

Fox, F. G. *Funky Butt Blues.* New Orleans: St. Expedite Press, 1994.

Gandolfo, Henri A. *Metairie Cemetery, an Historical Memoir.* New Orleans: Stewart Enterprises, 1981.

Gill, Donald. *Stories Behind New Orleans Street Names.* Chicago: Bonus Books, 1992.

Hannusch, Jeff. *I hear you knockin': the sound of New Orleans rhythm & blues.* Ville Platte, La: Swallow Publications, 1985.

Huber, Leonard V. *Clasped Hands: Symbolism in New Orleans Cemeteries.* Lafayette, La: Center for Louisiana Studies, 1982.

_____. *New Orleans: a Pictorial History.* New York: Crown, 1971.

BIBLIOGRAPHY (continued)

_____. *To Glorious Immortality: The Rise and Fall of the Girod Street Cemetery.* New Orleans: Alblen Books, 1961.

Kerouac, Jack. *On the Road.* New York: Penguin Books, 1991.

Klein, Victor. *New Orleans Ghosts.* New Orleans: Lycanthrope Press, 1993.

Saxon, Lyle. *Fabulous New Orleans.* New Orleans: Robert L. Crager, 1958.

_____. Louisiana Writers Program. *Gumbo Ya-Ya.* Boston: Houghton Mifflin, 1945.

Smith, Michael. *Mardi Gras Indians.* Gretna, La: Pelican Publishing Co, 1994.

Tallant, Robert. *Voodoo in New Orleans.* New York: Macmillan, 1946.

Taylor, Joe Gray . *Louisiana, a history.* New York: Norton, 1984.

Federal Writers Program. *Louisiana: A Guide to the State.* New York: Hastings House, 1971.

INDEX

CEMETERY   LOCATIONS

*Metairie -- 5100 Pontchartrain Boulevard
*St. Louis I -- Basin Street, between St. Louis and Conti
*St. Louis II -- North Claiborne Avenue, between St. Louis and
    Iberville
*St. Louis III -- 3421 Esplanade Avenue
*St. Roch #1 -- 1725 St. Roch Avenue
*Lafayette #2 -- Washington Avenue, between Loyola and
    Saratoga
*Cypress Grove -- 120 City Park Avenue
*Greenwood -- 5242 Canal Boulevard
*Holt -- 635 City Park Avenue
*St. Vincent de Paul -- 1322 Louisa Street
*Gates of Prayer #1 -- 4800 Canal Street
*Charity Hospital -- 5050 Canal Street
*Garden of Memories -- 4800 Airline Highway